JOB SATISFACTION SCALES
FOR
EFFECTIVE MANAGEMENT

THE AUTHOR

Dr. H.C. Ganguli, D.Phil, D.Litt (Calcutta), received his post-doctoral training at the Laboratory of Aviation Psychology, Ohio State University, Columbus, and in Student Counselling at the University of Minnesota. He established the Department of Psychology of the Delhi University in 1963 as Professor and Head. Earlier, he had worked in the Flight Safety Directorate of the Indian Air Force, at the Indian Institute of Technology, Kharagpur, and at the All-India Institute of Hygiene and Public Health, Calcutta.

He helped to develop the post-graduate Department of Psychology at the Tribhuvan University, Kathmandu, Nepal.

Amongst his other assignments, he was Senior Industrial Psychologist with the Iraq National Oil Company at Baghdad.

He is a Fellow of the Indian National Science Academy and has received awards like the Sandoz Award of the Indian Psychiatric Society and the Escorts Award of the Delhi Management Association. He is a Member of the Delhi Management Association.

Besides his many research papers, some of the books he has published are: *Industrial Productivity and Motivation - A Psychological Analysis* (Asia, Bombay-1961; Reprinted Allied, New Delhi - 1983). *Structure and Processes of Organization* (Asia - 1964; Reprinted Allied-1983). *Human Factor Aspects of Aircraft Noise* (Vikas, New Delhi - 1971). *Behavioural Research in Sexuality* (Vikas - 1988). His Report on An Organization Development School for the Iraq National Oil Company, Baghdad (printed by the INOC, Baghdad) may also be mentioned.

JOB SATISFACTION SCALES FOR EFFECTIVE MANAGEMENT

MANUAL FOR MANAGERS AND SOCIAL SCIENTISTS

H.C. GANGULI

Formerly of the All-India Institute of Hygiene and Public Health, Calcutta and Indian Institute of Technology, Kharagpur

Introduction by

Ishwar Dayal

Professor Emeritus
Management Development Institute
Gurgaon

CONCEPT PUBLISHING COMPANY, NEW DELHI

ISBN 81-7022-512-4

First Published 1994

Published and Printed by
Ashok Kumar Mittal
Concept Publishing Company
A/15-16, Commercial Block, Mohan Garden
NEW DELHI 110059 (India)

Laser type-set by
Printing Express
H-13, Bali Nagar
NEW DELHI 110015

DEDICATED TO
My Guru and Mentor
Dr Manthripragada Narasimha Rao,
M.B.B.S., Dr. P.H. (Harvard)
Professor of Physiological
and Industrial Hygiene (Retd.)
All India Institute
of Hygiene and
Public Health,
Calcutta
With Respect
and
Affection

CONTENTS

INTRODUCTION

Measurement is basic to effective management. Extremely useful work has been done in respect to measuring financial results, market related data, inventory, production, and many other managerial functions and processes. The measures of health of the human organisation have been comparatively more difficult to develop. Two types of measures have been tried. One is an index of significant areas of behaviour such as absenteeism, cases of indiscipline, trends in these and similar areas of end-behaviour. Quantitative indicators are easily available for such data. These are useful indicators but give limited measures of the health and the remedial actions necessary to improve the human side of the enterprise. Behaviour, as observed, is an expression of something that may be happening within the individual. Any positive or negative samples of behaviour are likely to be a symptom and not the cause. The manager has to know the reason of the particular behaviour in order to effectively manage it. The data about the human organisation have to provide an index of the inner dynamics or the process. Like a chemical process, one sees the final product but not what is taking place inside the test tube (in physical and biological sciences, we are increasingly beginning to see this as well). One has to derive the process from the observed behaviour. Remedial action would invariably require change in the process. We need to obtain data on the unobserved reactions that take place within the self. Hence instruments to measure behaviour would have to capture the inner dynamics.

An instrument to measure behaviour at work would have to take into account many considerations. The concept relating to the particular behaviour must be clear, Take Job Satisfaction for example. What does this phenomenon mean. For an individual, it should mean that something within him reacts favourably to the job and its environment. It is an overall *feeling* of being satisfied with the content and the context of work.

What he does, and the things around him, evoke certain positive feelings within him. Hence a measure of job satisfaction should be able to isolate this *feeling* and measure it. How does one arrive at this overall or a summary feeling of satisfaction. One can identify the various components of his job and measure each individually and add up these to arrive at an overall measure. Hence many scales include the intrinsic and the extrinsic elements of the job and obtain the level of satisfaction of the employee with each. And summation of all the elements provides an index of job satisfaction.

Elements of the job have to be identified. One method of doing this is to apply statistical methods such as factor analysis and identify factors that are critical to the situation. The second method is to analyse characteristics of the experience that give pleasure or pain. Prof. Ganguli in this book has used the first approach. Herzberg in his work has used the second approach. Both have advantages and disadvantages that have been extensively discussed in the job satisfaction literature.

Another consideration in developing a measure of job satisfaction is that the sum total of the various elements of the job do not necessarily reflect the *overall feeling* about the job. One can feel happy about many of the elements, yet, on the whole, feel dissatisfied. And the combination of elements for different people may be different, depending upon their own needs or predilections. The strength of one element can neutralise the effect of many other elements. The effect of these elements on individuals could also vary considerably. Some people may derive pleasure from relationships on the job, and others may derive that feeling from intrinsic factors in the job. Yet some others may seek satisfaction away from work. The measure of job satisfaction would have to achieve a viable balance between such differences. While interpreting data on job satisfaction, norms of the population would be needed. Scientific rigour in obtaining data and interpreting it is necessary to derive conclusions that a manager can use with confidence for managerial action. Whether sum total of parts represents the total feeling about job satisfaction, or not, is generally answered from field data. In conceptual terms, sum total of parts is not necessarily an index of the totality. At present, however, one has to rely on the empirical data on the subject. Intelligence was defined as that which the intelligence test measures. In the case of job satisfaction also, the scale that differentiates employees who are satisfied from those who are not, is a measure of job satisfaction. This, however, underscores that the scale has to be constructed with considerable care and standardised on the population.

A scale to measure job satisfaction has to be concerned with many other technical issues as well. The questions must convey the same meaning as intended. These have to be carefully tested independently. The scale should differentiate the level of response from one person to another. These have to be also tested independently.

The scale should be able to differentiate between the levels of satisfaction on the various elements in the scale. These have to be also tested independently. The scale should avoid duplicate measures of the same characteristic, otherwise the data would be corrupted.

The construction of a scale to measure job satisfaction has to be done with care, using statistical tests to know that it is reliable. Non-standard scales of job satisfaction may not give the data that the manager needs.

Prof. Ganguli has exercised all the care necessary for developing a scale for measuring job satisfaction at work. I am sure researchers and managers in organisations will find this contribution most valuable.

New Delhi
June 1993

ISHWAR DAYAL

PREFACE

Managers working in industries and scholars engaged in Ph.D. or project work have often requested me for a job satisfaction scale that can be used by them on their subjects. Lack of such a scale meant that the intending user had to improvise or standardise one of his own, which is time consuming and also not originally intended as part of the project. Therefore, I felt that I should provide in a single volume a set of scales which we have standardised over the past years and had published in different journals. The present work is the result.

The book is written from an applied point of view and for use by managers, administrators and other applied social scientists in psychology, sociology etc. on persons working in various organizations—industrial, business, scientific, governmental and so on.

The important features of the work are now summarised:

1. It has two scales for measuring overall satisfaction with the job—a long scale and a short scale.

2. Two other scales deal only with satisfaction with immediate superior from the technical and from the human relations point of view. Another scale deals with the employee's overall confidence in the employing organization.

3. The scales have been standardized in a comprehensive manner through item choice, item analysis, factor analysis and computation of reliability coefficients. Validity of scales has been appropriately discussed.

4. The user can apply these scales on individual subjects or groups and compute raw scores, convert these into standard scores and interpret the 'meaning' of the scores in terms of 'goodness' of satisfaction. The appropriate steps have been given and norms etc. provided.

5. An introductory chapter on some theories of job satisfaction is given and discussed to acquaint the reader with the type of thinking associated with job satisfaction.

6. Since this is essentially a user's work, all references have been omitted. Any standard text in industrial and organizational psychology can however provide the reader with such references.

7. The scales have been called employee attitude scales rather than job satisfaction scales as the term attitude is emotionally more neutral.

I am very grateful to Professor Ishwar Dayal who has read the book carefully and has made valuable suggestions. I thank Sri R.K.Gupta who has typed the manuscript with assiduous care. I also express my sincere thanks to Sri Dalip Singh, I.A.S. and Capt. N.K. Ganguli for help in photocopying the material. My wife has given me total moral support throughout the period of writing this work. I express my gratitude to her.

I express my sincere thanks to the **Concept Publishing Company** and to its proprietor and Managing Director, Sri Ashok Kumar Mittal, for full cooperation in publishing this work with care and speed.

It is my hope that the book shall prove useful to the readers.

August 31, 1993

H.C. GANGULI

CHAPTER I

THEORIES OF JOB SATISFACTION
An Overview

The Concept of Job Satisfaction

Historically speaking, the term 'job satisfaction' came into vogue in 1935 when Hoppock published his classic work *Job Satisfaction*. He defined job satisfaction as "any combination of psychological, physiological and environmental circumstances that cause a person truthfully to say, I am satisfied with my job". Thus job satisfaction is the verbal expression of an employee's evaluation of his work life.

There has been considerable confusion over the use of the term 'job satisfaction'. For example, in a number of studies conducted by the Survey Research Centre of the Michigan University at Ann Arbor, the term morale has been used synonymously with job satisfaction. "By morale in this paper we mean the employee's satisfactions and dissatisfactions with the work situation." (Mann and Pelz, 1945). Kornhauser (1949) also regards morale as meaning contentment or satisfaction of the worker with the job and the company. Fryer (1950) says that morale is individual well-being within the social set-up and tied to the social situation. On the other hand, writers like Blum (1949) regard morale as the feeling on the part of the worker of being accepted by and belonging to a group of employees through adherence to common goals and confidence in the desirability of these goals. Industrial morale is generated by the group and is a by-product of the group. Such a theory as of Blum is supported by many. For example, Schachter et al. (1951) in their discussion of the cohesiveness-morale theory, mention the close relation between the two concepts and their role in group productivity.

In the present work the two terms -- job satisfaction and employee morale—shall be used interchangeably and refer to the individual employee only.

Job satisfaction is thus an attitude which results from a balancing and summation of many specific likes and dislikes experienced in connection with the job. It is the employee's judgement of how well the job on the whole is satisfying his various needs. However, a global concept of job satisfaction is not warranted by findings from job satisfaction studies. Job satisfaction is not a single unified entity but is a multidimensional concept. It breaks down into such dimensions as intrinsic task satisfaction, attachment to the work group, satisfaction with superiors, identification with the company, satisfaction with security and income, chances of promotion etc.

Theories of Job Satisfaction

Five general orientations or theories towards understanding of job satisfaction are usually distinguished, all of which purport to describe the process by which job satisfaction is determined for individuals. These are: comparison theory, instrumentality theory, social influence theory, equity theory and the two-factor theory.

The comparison theory denies that job satisfaction is just an additive function of the objective outcomes from the job received by the individual. Rather, the magnitude of satisfaction is a function of the size of the discrepancy between the individual's standard and what the individual believes he or she is receiving from the job. The standard is considered by some as the individual's needs (Porter, 1962; Morse, 1953), and by others as his values (Locke,1976).

We have referred to this theory as the aspiration-achievement or expectation-achievement discrepancy theory of job satisfaction. However, the situation is complicated by the fact that aspiration and achievement are not independent of each other. Aspiration or expectations can be set by the minimum needs of the individual and/or by his current level of achievement of needs. It was noted for Calcutta industrial employees that for income expectation, "a majority of workers think in terms of a comfortable living for their family". Secondly, it was also noted that "correlation between present earnings and income expectation is always above 0.4" (Ganguli, 1957). It was concluded: "... a person's present earnings serve as a frame of reference by which he sets his aspirations."

Extending these findings on satisfaction with income to the general area of job satisfaction, we conclude that whereas it is undoubtedly true that job satisfaction is determined by a comparison of the desired standard and perception of the achieved level, the standard itself is not a fixed but a 'moving' standard, linked in a significant way to the achievement level. This explains an often noted phenomenon of increased employee dissatisfaction following an increment in wages. What happens very often in such cases is that the wage increase has led to a more than proportionate increase in income aspiration, resulting in increased achievement-aspiration discrepancy after the wage increase than what it was before.

The instrumentality theory postulates that individuals assess their satisfaction with jobs by considering the extent to which the jobs lead to valued outcomes. It is assumed here that each individual has a set of judgements about how much he values certain outcomes such as pay, promotion, good working condition etc. The person then estimates the extent to which holding the job leads to these valued outcomes. His job satisfaction then results from a summation of outcomes or instrumentalities obtained multiplied by the valences of these outcomes.

The basic assumption of the social influence theory of job satisfaction is that individuals may come into new jobs not knowing how satisfied they will be with these. They look around, see others like themselves who are satisfied or dissatisfied with these, and are then influenced by these observations. Thus people decide how satisfied they are with their jobs not by processing all types of information about themselves but by observing others on similar jobs and making inferences about their satisfactions (Salancik and Pfeffer, 1977). Thus satisfaction is more a product of self-perception and social perceptions, rather than determined by intrinsic characteristic of the job. An individual simply infers a level of his or her personal satisfaction by their perception of other's satisfactions.

The equity theory, according to Adam (1965), holds that people make a cognitive comparison of their contribution to a work situation (their inputs) and the things they get out of it (their outcomes) with those of other people. Among the important inputs are: skills and knowledge; experience; time on the job; etc. Outcomes include pay, status and job level etc. Satisfaction becomes a ratio of output to input.

Inequity exists for a person when he perceives that the ratio of his outcomes to inputs and ratio of other's outcomes to their inputs are unequal. Equity exists when the ratio of outcome to input of an individual as perceived by him equals similar ratios of other employees. Inequity may thus favour the individual making the comparison or it may favour the relevant others. Imbalance or inequity, meaning perceived imbalance between effort and reward, is experienced as a psychological tension leading to behavioural changes towards restoration of balance or equity. Thus the individual may change his effort level and performance or may seek a change in the reward received.

Herzberg (Herzberg, Mausner and Snyderman, 1959) proposed that job satisfaction is derived from two sets of factors. The first set associated with positive feelings about the job and related to the content of the work itself has been called the intrinsic content or motivation factors. These satisfier factors include achievement, recognition, the work itself, responsibility and advancement. The second set of factors has been labelled hygiene factors or dissatisfiers. These factors do not induce satisfaction; they simply prevent dissatisfaction. These factors are external to the work itself and include company policies and practices, supervision, salary, interpersonal relations with coworkers and working conditions.

The two-factor theory states that the hygiene factors can usually dissatisfy if they are not present in sufficient amounts. At best, these can bring a person to a psychologically neutral point (no job dissatisfaction) or create a zero level of motivation. Such factors as good supervision, adequate salaries, positive degree of peer interaction etc. will prevent dissatisfaction but will not develop employee motivation for work. The motivation is a function of the satisfiers or motivators like sense of achievement, advancement etc.

Ten years of research and experience with the two-factor

theory have led to serious doubts about the validity of this theory. For example, a given job factor can cause satisfaction to one person and lead to dissatisfaction in another person. This difference in individual reactions is often due to their previous job levels, age, sex, formal education, cultural background etc. The Herzberg theory is an over-simplification of the complex relationship between motivation and satisfaction and the sources of job satisfaction and dissatisfaction.

Concluding Remarks

1. The above theories of job satisfaction deal with causes of satisfaction and dissatisfaction and not with nature of job satisfaction *per se.* This latter would involve taking into consideration personality factors other than needs only, like ego-strength, attitude towards work, sense of inner hostility, ethicality etc.
2. In these theories four parameters are involved: (i) The person's own needs and values; (ii) The person's education, ability, experience, skill etc. that determine his contributions to the job; (iii) Reward the employer gives to him; and (iv) Rewards given to other employees in the organization.
3. The different satisfaction theories take up different combinations of these factors and base their theories only on the parameters they choose.
4. In our opinion, the theories are not exclusive of each other but overlapping. Further, operationally, the validity and applicability of the theories depend on the career stage of the employee and other factors inside and outside the organization.
5. Let us illustrate point 4 above. An employee says he is dissatisfied with the job and intends to quit. The reason given is non-recognition of his qualifications and being bypassed in promotion by subordinates. Here a sense of inequity (equity theory) and the social influence theory (promotion to others and not to himself) are operating. On close questioning, the person may admit that he has no complaints as such about his pay, working conditions or even personal promotion rules. That is, the instrumentality theory is fulfilled. What he bothers about is promotion to another person, less senior or less qualified. In rapidly expanding organizations, the social influence theory of job satisfaction assumes much centrality.

On the other hand, when a person is seeking entry into a job and for sometime to come, personal factors marked as (i) and (ii) and rewards from the employer, (iii) in para 1 above, shall operate. The person assesses the extent to which his valued outcomes like pay, security, nature of work etc. fulfil his expectations. Both summation effects of the instrumentality theory and the reward-expectation of the comparison theory determine his satisfaction now. In the initial years at least his job satisfaction will continue to be determined thus, and till such time when some other salient social or other factors intervene.

6. In any analysis of individual cases of satisfaction-dissatisfaction, any single theory claiming to cover all cases fail. Very often, a single factor becomes prominent and suddenly converts, for example, a middling satisfied person into a dissatisfied grumbler seeking an alternate job or lateral transfer or just gets 'burnt out', emotionally exhausted and continues with the job as an 'apathetic' worker. Occasionally, the employee may develop a sense of exaggerated importance about his abilities and if he has a strong sense of inner hostility, he may engage in pathological clique formation in the department, sometimes directed against the very person who had built him up and had been his mentor and teacher. On a conventional job satisfaction scale, this person would have rated himself as satisfied and his performance satisfactory up to that point.

   To understand these cases, one needs to know any 'critical incident' in his life at the time as well as the psychic forces within him. For example, in the last case above, his being sent abroad by the institution may have released his hitherto supressed hunger for power, his lack or ethicality and moral values and his skill in organizing informal cliques. The spouse is usually a factor in most such cases. None of the satisfaction theories explains these cases satisfactorily.

7. Therefore, when the term job satisfaction is used, the question should be asked: Job satisfaction for whom, working in what type of organization and under what socio-economic-technological climate in the society. Each of the theories presented above is valid up to a point, for a person at a particular stage in his career, and working in a certain socio-economic and technological climate.

We conclude that each theory embodies a partial truth, but none covers the entire spectrum of job satisfaction-dissatisfaction. A perceptive and discerning manager or researcher should opt for that particular theory which enables him to understand his empirical data adequately.

References

Adams, J.S. Inequality in Social Exchange. In Berkowitz, L. (ed). *Advances in Experimental Psychology*, Vol. 2, Academic Press, New York, 1965.

Blum, M.L. *Industrial Psychology and its Social Foundations*. Harper and Brothers, New York, 1949.

Fryer, D.H. Morale, In *Handbook of Applied Psychology*, Vol. I, by Fryer *et al.* (ed). Henry and Rinehart, New York, 1950.

Ganguli, H.C. Some Factors Influencing Income Aspiration. *J. of Applied Psychology*, 41, 1, 1957.

Herzberg, F., Mausner, B. and Snyderman, B.B. *The Motivation to Work*. John Wiley, New York, 1959.

Kornhauser, A. (ed). *Psychology of Labor-Management Relations*. Industrial Relations Research Association, U.S.A., 1949.

Locke, E.A. Nature and Causes of Job Satisfaction. In Dunnette, M. (ed). *Handbook of Industrial and Organizational Psychology*, 1976.

Mann, F.C. and Pelz, D.C. *A Comparison of High and Low Morale Work Groups*. Survey Research Center, Ann Arbor, 1945.

Morse, Nancy C. *Satisfaction in White Collar Job*. Institute for Social Research, Ann Arbor, 1953.

Porter, L.W. Job Attitudes in Management, *J. of Applied Psychology*, 375-384, 46, 1962.

Salancik, G.R. and Pfeffer, J. *An Examination of Need Satisfaction Models of Job Satisfaction*. Administrative Science quarterly, 427-456, 22, 1977.

Schachter, S. *et al.* An Experimental Study of Cohesiveness and Productivity. *Human Relations*, 222-239, IV, 1951.

CHAPTER II

SHORT EMPLOYEE ATTITUDE SCALE FOR JOB SATISFACTION (SEA SCALE)

I

Standardisation Sample: A 40-item scale called the Master Employment Attitude Scale or MEA Scale and the 12-item scale—Short Employee Attitude Scale (SEA Scale), have been developed on a sample of 380 workers, all males, of a Calcutta engineering factory. Its major manufacturing item was sewing machines and it had a work-force of 680. Thirty workers were selected on the basis of the random number table from each of the 12 manufacturing departments and an extra 20 from a few sub-sections. 344 were Hindus and 309 were Bengalees, that is, natives of Calcutta. Their mean age was 27.9 ± 6.4 and length of service 6.4 ± 2.4 years. By education, 200 had studied up to the primary standard, 63 up to the middle standard, 69 up to High School standard, whereas 48 were illiterates. In this group of 380, there were 223 machine operators working on the lathe, capstan etc. (129 skilled and 94 semi-skilled). 145 were skilled craftsmen like tool inspectors, and 12 were helpers. 269 workers or about 71% of the whole group were members of the labour union and 111 workers were unattached non-members.

II

Master Employee Attitude Scale (MEA Scale)

Originally, the Master Employee Attitude Scale (MEA Scale) consisting of 40 items was developed and the SEA Scale was extracted from this. The steps in the MEA scale development were the following:

1. Likert's attitude scaling principle of summated ratings was adopted.
2. On the basis of non-directive interviews with 40 workers and three pre-tests on 10 workers each as well as scanning of relevant literature, items were collected. Forty of these referred to different satisfaction areas. These 40 items constituted the preliminary scale and item analysed.
3. The 40 items were written out carefully with usual precautions regarding wordings etc. Thirty-one items had 5 response alternatives each and 9 items 3 each.
4. Areas of job satisfaction covered were:

Intrinsic nature of work	:	6
Wage and security	:	12
Supervision	:	10
Company Policies and Practices	:	12

No subject referred to work groups. Even direct questioning did not. All said they are happy with colleagues and can work with anyone.

5. One hundred subjects were used as the standardisation sample for validation of the scale. Sigma scores were used for the response alternatives instead of simple 1 to 5 scores. The score distribution for 100 Ss was tested for normalcy by Pearson's test for goodness of fit through the *P* coefficient. Chi-square was 6.927 and *n* of 8. Probability falls between 0.7 and 0.5, which indicates 'excellent' fit.
6. Validity of the Scale has been tested through the method of internal consistency and not the method of external judgement which is laborious (Vernon, 1952). Item analysis was done by the *D* or Discrimination values of each item with 25 top-

scoring and 25 low-scoring subjects as the two criterion groups. *D* values of 35 items were significant at one per cent level, of 2 items at five per cent level and only three items were not discriminating significantly between the two criteria group.

7. For reason of content representativeness, these three items have not been dropped and all the 40 items are thus included in the MEA scale.
8. The mean score for the group of 100 on the MEA Scale was 119.9±16.0, and maximum possible range of scores 49 to 191. The odd-even reliability of the scale is *r* (*o-e*): 0.797 and with Spearman-Brown's correction, 0.887.
9. The MEA scale is not reproduced here.

III

Standardization of SEA Scale

A 40-item scale is too long and time consuming for practical use. A short employee attitude scale, herein called the SEA scale, consisting of 12 items has therefore been derived from the original 40-item MEA scale. The logic and the steps are given below:

1. It was felt that the scale should be sufficiently short for use in industrial organizations. However, since length of a scale is positively correlated with reliability, the scale should be long enough to give a minimum acceptable reliability.
2. The different satisfaction areas should be represented by the items in the scale.
3. A 12-item scale was decided to be of optimum length.
4. For the selection of these 12 items out of the larger pool of 40 items of the MEA scale, the following was done:

   (a) All items from the pool of 40 having a *D*-value of 1.0 or higher were selected. These were 24 in number.
   (b) The correlation of each of these 24 items with total score on 40 items were calculated. *A* 'good' item should have not only high *D*-value but also high correlation with the total score.
   (c) The 12 items selected from the 24 items were on the following basis : Ten items with *r* values of 0.5 or more selected. One item with *r* value of .468 and on job

security and another with *r* of .448 and on Section Supervisor have been included to give coverage to security and superviory functions.

Reliability of SEA

The satisfaction score based on the 12-item MEA Scale correlated highly (r =0.95) with the score on the 40-item MEA Scale. The MEA Scale itself had a reliability of 0.89 and the high correlation between scores of MEA and SEA Scales support the reliability of the latter. The SEA Scale is thus a good surrogate of the MEA Scale with the added merit of short length and consequently ease in administration and scoring.

The odd-even reliability of the 12-item SEA Scale after Spearman-Brown correction is 0.79 (N =250).

Validity of SEA: Checking the validity of an attitude scale is often very difficult largely due to the lack of a proper criterion whose relation with the attitude in question is fully known in all aspects. That is why Vernon (1952) says: "We may claim that when reasonable precautions are taken in constructing the test, and in obtaining coopration from the testees, the validity should be good. And there is a large measure of scattered evidence supporting this conclusion". The two most important factors that affect validity of a test are: (i) the internal consistency of the test, and (ii) the scoring of responses and the certainty that a given response represents favourable rather than unfavourable attitude toward the issue involved (Murphy, Murphy and Newcomb, 1937). Careful steps have been taken in securing honest cooperation of the subjects and towards giving him every facility to discuss and state his own attitude. The product-moment correlations between the 12 items with each other and with the final score based on these 12 items are given in Table 1. Table 1 shows that the double criteria of low inter-item correlation and high item-total score correlation are met adequately by the SEA Scale. High and significant *D*-values of each of the 12 items and the data presented in Table 1 support the validity of the scale. It is thus reasonable to assume that the SEA Scale yields data that are scientifically as accurate as is possible for attitudinal data and the scale is acceptably valid.

Table 2 gives the SEA Scale.

Table 1

Inter-Item and Item-vs-Total Score Correlations for the 12-item

SEA Scale (N =100)

1	2	3	4	5	6	7	8	9	10	11	12	Final Morale score
1	.31	.41	.35	.40	.14	.16	.42	.29	.30	.46	.27	.73
2		.29	.30	.22	.23	.14	.37	.68	.44	.42	.29	.60
3			.39	.35	.48	.27	.36	.57	.47	.33	.46	.76
4				.24	.20	.10	.40	.39	.27	.47	.39	.66
5					.18	.35	.37	.25	.27	.28	.11	.52
6						.27	.40	.59	.47	.12	.26	.60
7							.25	.40	.36	.12	.13	.45
8								.38	.32	.27	.34	.78
9									.55	.35	.27	.70
10										.41	.27	.37
11											.29	.60
12												.54

IV

Table 2

SHORT EMPLOYEE ATTITUDE SCALE
(SEA Scale)

1. Is there any other work you think you would be able to do better than your present work?

*.......3 I cannot say for certain
........4 I do this better than I could do most
........1 Almost any other work I think I would be able to do better
........2 There are a few others which I could do better
........5 I am best at this work.

2. Do you think that the organization's policy is to overdrive the worker and get the maximum out of him ?

........1 Strongly agreed
........2 Agreed

* The numerical values of the response alternatives should be removed in actual use.

........5 Strongly disagreed
........3 Undecided
........4 Disagreed

3. How satisfied are you with the chances you have in increasing your income in this organisation
........5 Very well satisfied
........1 Very dissatisfied
........3 So so
........4 Fairly well satisfied
........2 Somewhat dissatisfied

4. Do you believe that so long as you work efficiently you will not lose your job ?
........1 Strongly disagreed
........2 Disagreed
........3 Undecided
........5 Strongly agreed
........4 Agreed

5. How reasonable is your immediate superior in the work he expects from you ?
........2 Not very reasonable
........4 Fairy reasonable
........5 Very reasonable
........3 About average
........1 Quite unreasonable

6. How much satisfied are you with the general supervision of your section/department ?
........4 Satisfied
........3 About average
........2 Dissatisfied
........1 Very dissatisfied
........5 Very satisfied

7. How much interest your superior or "section in-charge" takes in your general welfare ?
........4 Much interest
........3 Some interest
........2 Very little interest

8. Are you satisfied with the running of the factory canteen, housing, retirement and other non-medical benefits ?

........3 Undecided
........4 Satisfied
........2 Dissatisfied

9. Do you believe that the company/organization is sympathetic to and appreciative of the worker's point of view ?

........1 It is definitely not true
........2 In general it is not true
........3 In some cases they are sympathetic, in some not
........4 I believe this to be more or less correct
........5 I strongly believe this

10. Do you feel that the company satisfies the reasonable demands of the employees

........5 Strongly agreed
........4 Agreed
........1 Strongly disagreed
........2 Disagreed
........3 So so

11. Is it that this organization is a better place to work than other neighbouring units?

........4 To a large extent, it is
........5 It definitely is
........3 It is about the same
........1 It definitely is not
........2 To a large extent, it is not

12. How satisfied you feel about the progress you have made in this company up to now?

........5 Very satisfied
........4 Satisfied
........2 Dissatisfied
........3 So so
........1 Very dissatisfied

V

Scoring for SEA Scale

1. The total score of a subject is the simple addition of the score values of the response alternatives checked. The individual has to check all the 12 items; no omission is allowed. In case he cannot make up his mind about a particular question, he is required to check the middle position carrying score of 3.

2. Areas covered by the 12 items are as follows :

Nature of work	:	1
Pay and Security	:	2, 3, 4
Superior	:	5, 6, 7
Company Policies and Practice	:	8, 9, 10, 11, 12

3. The mean and SD of job satisfaction scores of 380 workers on the SEA scale was 37.1.± 5.37. The minimum and maximum possible scores in this scale are 14 and 58.

4. Odd-even reliability of SEA after Spearman-Brown correction: 0.79.

5. For prupose of intra-group and inter-group comparisons of satisfaction scores derived from different scales, it is not possible to use raw scores derived directly from the Scale. Standard scores in lieu of raw scores permit such comparisons. Therefore, the raw scores on the SEA scale from the 380 workers have been converted into standard scores with a mean of 50 and SD of 10 and presented in Table 3. Norms for evaluating 'goodness' or quality of satisfaction from standard scores are given later.

Table 3

Test Scores and Standard Scores on the Short Employee Attitude Scale (SEA Scale)
(N = 380)

Test Score	Standard Score	Test Score	Standard Score
14	7	36	48
15	9	37	50
16	11	38	52
17	12	39	53
18	14	40	55
19	16	41	57
20	18	42	59
21	20	43	61
22	22	44	63
23	24	45	65
24	26	46	66
25	27	47	68
26	29	48	70
27	31	49	72
28	33	50	74
29	35	51	76
30	37	52	78
31	39	53	79
32	40	54	81
33	42	55	83
34	44	56	85
35	46	57	87
		58	89

References

1. Murphy, G., Murphy, L.B. and Newcomb, T.M. *Experimental Social Psychology*. Harper and Bros., New York, 1937.
2. Vernon, P.E. *Assessment of Psychological Qualities by Verbal Methods.* Industrial Relations Research Board Report No. 83. London, 1952.

CHAPTER III

LONG EMPLOYEE ATTITUDE SCALE FOR JOB SATISFACTION
(E-A SCALE)

From the 40-item MEA scale discussed earlier, a 26-item scale for measuring work satisfaction of Nepalese educated women employees was standardised by Dr Rita Shresthya and the present author. This scale is of medium length and is somewhat time consuming. But it has norms for highly educated samples and has greater coverage of the satisfaction subareas. Secondly, as the standardization sample were all women, the norm would be directly applicable for educated women employees. Since the master scale from which items for the E-A scale has been drawn is the MEA Scale, the scale is applicable both to Nepalese and Indian samples.

The standardization sample consisted of 240 female subjects, 80 college teachers, 80 government employees, and 80 bank employees, all from Kathmandu. 161 were in the age group 26 to 37 years, 28 between 20 to 25 and 51 from 38 to 55. Forty-five had no college degrees, whereas 59 were graduates and 136 held post-graduate degrees. 167 were married women and 5 divorcees, with 68 unmarried. The length of service ranged from 4 to 21 years with 78 having 4 years or less of service, 52 between 5 to 8 years and 56 between 9 to 12. Income range for the group was from Nepalese Rs 645 to Rs 3444 and 210 were drawing monthly salaries of Rs 2044 or less. Designations of the subjects were:

College teachers: Reader -6; Lecturer -35; Asstt Lecturer -39

Bank employees: Officers -25; Below Officer rank -55

Govt employees: Officers -29; Below Officer rank-51.

The 26 items of the scale were drawn from the items given in the MEA scale on the basis of *d*-values of the items and their representativeness for different subareas of satisfaction. Likert's method of summated ratings of scaling was used. Twenty-five items had five response alternatives each and one 3 alternatives; scoring was in the direction of higher number for better satisfaction. The work satisfaction score of an employee was the sum of the scores of the alternatives the subject checked for the 26 items. The score range was 129(25×5+4) to 27(25×1+2).

The scale items cover the following six dimensions of job satisfaction: Work itself; Pay and other financial benefits; Promotional and training opportunities; Job security; Management/ Supervision; and Colleagues/Co-workers.

The 26 items of the E-A scale are reproduced in Table 4.

Administration, scoring and interpretation of the E-A Scale are done as for the SEA Scale.

Table 4

EMPLOYEE ATTITUDE SCALE
(The E-A Scale)

1. Does your job give you a chance to do the things you feel you do the best (not just liking the job)?

*.......4 Agreed
........3 Undecided
........2 Disagreed
........5 Strongly agreed
........1 Strongly disagreed

2. How satisfied are you with the allotment of work in your section/department?

........1 Very dissatisfied
........2 Dissatisfied
........5 Very satisfied
........4 Satisfied
........3 Undecided

3. How satisfied are you with your present salary?

* Numerical values of all response alternatives should be removed in use with candidates.

.......1 Very dissatisfied
.......5 Completely satisfied
.......3 Neither satisfied nor dissatisfied
.......4 Fairly well satisfied
.......2 Dissatisfied

4. What are your chances of being given a better type of job?
......1 No chance
......5 Very good chances
......4 Fair chances
......3 Cannot say
......2 Small chances

5. Do you believe that so long as you work efficiently you will not lose your job?
......1 Strongly disagreed
......2 Disagreed
......3 Undecided
......5 Strongly agreed
......4 Agreed

6. How reasonable is your immediate superior in the work he expects from you?
.......2 Not very reasonable
.......4 Fairly reasonable
.......5 Very reasonable
.......3 About average
.......1 Quite unreasonable

7. How much satisfied are you with the general supervision of your section/department?
.......4 Satisfied
.......3 About average
.......2 Dissatisfied
.......1 Very dissatisfied
.......5 Very satisfied

8. Are you satisfied that the people you work with give proper recognition to your work?
.......4 Agreed
.......2 Disagreed

.......5 Strongly agreed
.......1 Strongly disagreed
.......3 Undecided

9. My superior encourages me to offer suggestions for improvements in my section/department.
.......3 Undecided
.......2 Disagreed
.......1 Strongly disagreed
.......4 Agreed
.......5 Strongly agreed

10. Do you believe that the company/organization is sympathetic to and appreciative of the employee's point of view?
.......1 It is definitely not true
.......2 In general it is not true
.......3 In some cases they are sympathetic, in some not
.......4 I believe this to be more or less correct
.......5 I strongly believe this

11. Do you prefer to work with your present colleagues?
.......5 Strongly agreed
.......4 Agreed
.......1 Strongly disagreed
.......2 Disagreed
.......3 Uncertain

12. Do you think that the organization's policy is to over-drive the worker and get the maximum out of him?
.......1 Strongly agreed
.......2 Agreed
.......5 Strongly disagreed
.......3 Undecided
.......4 Disagreed

13. How satisfied are you with the method of allocation of your increments?
.......3 Neither satisfied nor dissatisfied
.......4 Satisfied
.......1 Completely dissatisfied
.......5 Completely satisfied

.......2 Dissatisfied

14. Do you feel your superior gives reasonable attention to your suggestions as regards method of work, equipment, books etc.?

.......2 Disagreed
.......1 Strongly disagreed
.......5 Strongly agreed
.......4 Agreed
.......3 Undecided

15. Do you feel that this organization treats its employees worse than other organizations?

.......2 Agreed
.......5 Strongly disagreed
.......4 Disagreed
.......3 So so
.......1 Strongly agreed

16. Is there any other work you think you would be able to do better than your present work?

.......3 I cannot say for certain
.......4 I do this better than I could do most
.......1 Almost any other work I think I would be able to do better
.......2 There are a few others which I could do better
.......5 I am best at this work.

17. Do you think that your income is somewhat larger than what you would have got in other similar organization?

.......1 Very much less
.......2 Somewhat less
.......3 About the same
.......5 Very much larger
.......4 Somewhat larger

18. How satisfied are you with the chances of promotion in your department/organization?

.......2 Dissatisfied
.......1 Strongly dissatisfied
.......4 Satisfied

.......5 Strongly satisfied
.......3 Undecided

19. How satisfied are you with the personal development, training and quality improvement programme in this organization?
.......3 Undecided
.......4 Satisfied
.......5 Very satisfied
.......2 Dissatisfied
.......1 Very dissatisfied

20. What is the relation in this organization between the union (or staff association) and the management?
.......5 Very good
.......4 Good
.......1 Very bad
.......3 Middling
.......2 Bad

21. If you are given the same type of job under same terms and conditions in a different organization, would you quit?
.......1 Always
.......5 Never
.......2 Probably
.......4 May not quit
.......3 Cannot say

22. How adequately the existing leave rules cover your average requirements?
.......2 These are not adequate for our purpose
.......3 Though these are not quite adequate, I do not have much to complain about these
.......4 These are satisfactorily adequate for our purpose

23. Do you feel you are given maximum facilities for doing your work properly?
.......1 We never get any facility
.......2 Mostly we do not get facilities
.......4 We get most of the facilities
.......3 We get about fifty-fifty
.......5 We get every facility

24. Are you satisfied with the running of the factory canteen, housing, retirement and other non-medical benefits?
.......3 Undecided
.......4 Satisfied
.......2 Dissatisfied
.......1 Very dissatisfied
.......5 Very satisfied

25. How satisfied are you with the chances you have in increasing your income in this organisation?
.......5 Very well satisfied
.......1 Very dissatisfied
.......3 So so
.......4 Fairly well satisfied
.......2 Somewhat dissatisfied

26. Taking all things into consideration, how satisfied are you with your service here:
.......2 Not satisfied
.......5 Very satisfied
.......4 Satisfied
.......3 Partly satisfied, partly dissatisfied
.......1 Not at all satisfied

The reliability of the scale using test-retest method was: r=0.90. Odd-even reliability after using Spearman-Brown's correction was: r=0.81. Validity of the scale was checked through the internal consistency method, that is, item analysis showing low correlations between items and high correlations between item score and total test score. This item analysis was done on the basis of a correlation matrix computed from data of first 100 subjects.

For purpose of intra-group and inter-group comparisons of satisfaction scores of different subjects, on the same or different scales, the actual satisfaction scores for 240 educated female employees have been converted into standard scores with a mean of 50 and standard deviation of 10 (Table 5).

Table 5

Test Scores and Standard Scores in the 26-item Employee Attitude Scale
N= 240 (E-A Scale)

Test score	Standard score	Test score	Standard score
35 (or less)	15	56	32
36	16	57	32
37	16	58	33
38	17	59	34
39	18	60	35
40	19	61	36
41	20	62	36
42	20	63	37
43	21	64	38
44	22	65	39
45	23	66	40
46	24	67	40
47	24	68	41
48	25	69	42
49	26	70	43
50	27	71	44
51	28	72	44
52	28	73	45
53	29	74	46
54	30	75	47
55	31	76	48
77	48	92	60
78	49	93	61
79	50	94	62
80	51	95	63
81	52	96	64
82	52	97	65
83	53	98	65
84	54	99	66
85	55	100	67
86	56	101	68
87	56	102	68
88	57	103	69
89	58	104	70
90	59	105	71
91	60	106 +	72

CHAPTER IV

VALIDATION OF JOB SATISFACTION SCALES BY ABSENTEEISM DATA

In certain cases the validity of attitude scales are checked against certain objective criterion, performance on which is supposed to have some relation to the attitude in question. Validity of employee satisfaction scales may be checked against participation measures (Bradshaw and Krughan, 1950) such as labour turnover, job tenure rate, different types of absenteeism, lateness, ratings by supervisors, productivity, grievances etc.

It was decided to find out how does absenteeism correlate with job satisfaction scores. Therefore absenteeism data were collected for the 380 workers in a light engineering factory for the 12-month period preceding the investigation and their satisfaction scores obtained from the 40-item MEA and 12-item SEA scales. Information was also sought regarding the nature of leave, reasons for the leave taken and number of times leave taken.

Tables 6 and 7 give correlations between morale scores and different types of absenteeism. In Table 6, the morale scores are based on responses to the 40 statements of the MEA scale and in Table 7, on the shorter scale of 12 highly discriminating items in the SEA scale.

Table 6

Correlations between Morale Scores (from 40-item MEA Scale) and Different Types of Absenteeism (N=100)

Correlation between Morale and	'r'
1. Total absenteeism	–0.13
2. Short medical leave (each of less than 3 days duration)	0.10
3. No. of times short medical leave taken	0.15
4. Total absence less long medical leave	0.09
5. Leave without pay	–0.08
6. Leave without pay less long medical leave without pay	0.07

Table 7

Correlations between Morale Scores (from SEA Scale: 12 items) and Different Types of Absenteeism

Correlation between Morale and	*N*	'r'
1. Total absenteeism	353	–0.43
2. No. of times leave taken	353	0.02
3. Short medical leave	169	0.06
4. No. of times short medical leave taken	169	0.08
5. Total absence less long medical leave	341	0.01
6. Leave without pay	350	–0.01

In the above tables, the only correlation that is significant is the one between total absenteeism and morale score based on the short SEA scale, –0.43. Poorer the job satisfaction, higher the total absenteeism.

Kerr (1951) deprecates the use of absenteeism as a unitary variable. He asserts that it is a non-unitary variable and "total absenteeism either is unrelated or 'unexpectedly' related to job satisfaction". He determined job satisfaction indices from 'tear ballots' (Kerr,1948) and found that it correlates –0.51 with total absenteeism and –0.44 with unexcused absenteeism.

To test this in India is difficult. Most employers do not keep records of excused and unexcused absenteeisms separately. But it is perhaps true that morale may relate more closely to some aspects of absenteeism than others or even total absenteeism. The nature of work, of supervision, method of wages and incentive payments and general quality of functioning of the organisation are some of the factors affecting absenteeism. Therefore, in dealing with absenteeism figures, the investigators may face 'unexpected' results. In connection with Kerr's results, it seems that the 'tear-ballot' system of getting satisfaction index itself needs further theoretical justification, for the only advantages of the system seem to be that it enables the respondents to remain anonymous and also saves them the bother of writing.

Brodman (1945) in two papers on emotional maladjustments suggested that such maladjustments which bears considerable relation to poor morale is best reflected in leaves taken for short durations (e.g. of less than 3 days) on medical ground. While this seems quite logical, values in Table 7 (and also in Table 6) do not support it. This suggestion is however worth pursuing.

Conclusion

A correlation of –0.43 substantiates the practice of many psychologists to test the validity of attitude scales by correlating it with absenteeism data. But as already mentioned, 'unexpected' results may be obtained when dealing with absenteeism figures. Actually, as pointed out by Murphy and Newcomb earlier, a valid attitude scale may be obtained if (i) internal consistency is ensured and (ii) the scoring is such that there is no confusion about a particular response representing favourable or unfavourable attitude toward the concerned issue.

References

Bradshaw, F.F. and Krughan, H.E. Industrial Morale. In Fryer *et al.* (ed). *Handbook of Applied Psychology*, Henry and Rinehart, New York, 1950.

Brodman, K. Absenteeism, Working Efficiency and Emotional Maladjustments, *Industrial Medicine*, 1, 14, 1945.

Kerr, W. *et al.*, Absenteeism, Turnover, and Morale in a Metals Fabrication Factory. *Occupational Psychology*, p. 50, XXV, 1951.

Kerr, W. On the Validity and Reliability of the Job Satisfaction Tear Ballot, *J. of Applied Psychology*, p. 275, 32, 1948.

CHAPTER V

SCALES FOR ASSESSING CONFIDENCE IN COMPANY AND IN SUPERVISION

I

Introduction

As a result of some recent studies in industrial morale, the global concept of morale has been found to be untenable. The hypothesis that worker morale is not a single unified entity but a multidimensional concept is more and more coming to the forefront. The term morale is given here an individual-organic emphasis and is used synonymously with job satisfaction of the worker.

The best way to isolate and identify the different morale dimensions is by factor analysis. This is what is reported here.

II

The Study

A morale survey was made by the author in an important electric fan manufacturing concern of Calcutta. This factory produces more than 29% of total fans manufactured in India and had 1,890 workers on its roll. The survey involved all the 550 workers in the foundry shop, the machine shop and one assembly shop. The method of study was the sample interview survey type. The study was conducted on the basis of an attitude scale constructed on the principle of summated ratings developed by Likert. This scale had 41 items; 32 of these were 5-point statements and 9, 3-point statements. It was constructed on the basis of initial exploratory interviews with 40 workers and four pretests. This scale contains all the items that were found to be significant and meaningful for these workers and nothing besides.

The statements had fixed alternative answers and the relevant response alternatives were checked by the investigator during an open non-directional interview with the worker. The usual precautions in the framing of these items, and conduct of the interviews for ensuring the validity of results were taken.

III

The Factor Analysis

Hotelling and Kelly's method of principal components and Thurstone's centroid method represent the two major methods of factor analysis. Thurstone's centroid solution has the advantage of making no assumption regarding the independence of the factors and also yields more consistent factors. So this method has been adopted for analysing the attitudinal data obtained from the above survey.

The factor analysis was conducted with only 23 of the 41 items as otherwise the task would have been very laborious. These 23 items were selected for their 'goodness' as judged from their discrimination values or *d*-values. The *d*-values were calculated from two-criterion groups made up of 50 most satisfied or high morale workers and 50 least satisfied or low morale workers in a larger group of 175 workers, the satisfication or dissatisfaction of the worker being indicated by his score on the full preliminary scale of 41 items the *d*-values for 38 of these items were positive and significant. Seventeen out of the 23 items selected for factor analysis had the highest *d*-values. The other six items have been included not on the strength of their *d*-values (which however were positive and significant) but in order to give representation to some specific aspects, namely, attitude towards the job content and satisfaction with pay increases and the welfare activities of the company.

Table 8 gives these 23 attitudinal items. Table 9 gives the correlation matrix of the 23 items based on data from 175 workers.

Table 8

Attitudinal Items included in Factor Analysis

1. there are some other work I would be able to do better than the work I do now.
2. like the job on the whole.
3. the company's policy is to overdrive the worker and get the maximum out of him.
4. satisfied with present earnings.
5. income is somewhat larger than what I would have got in other similar factories.
6. satisfied with the method of allocation of increments.
7. satisfied with chances of increasing income at this factory.
8. shall not lose job so long as I work efficiently.
9. satisfied with my chances of getting a better type of job.
10. immediate superior is reasonable in the work he expects from me.
11. he gives reasonable attention to suggestions regarding method of work, tools etc.
12. he is my own man.
13. satisfied with the general supervision of my section.
14. satisfied with the allotment of work in the section.
15. my section in-charge is good in the way he handles the workers.
16. I am given maximum facilities for doing my work properly.
17. satisfied with the running of the factory canteen.
18. factory dispensary gives satisfactory service.
19. the existing leave rules cover my average requirements adequately.
20. I feel that this company treats its workers worse than other companies.
21. the company is sympathetic to and appreciative of the worker's point of view.
22. this factory is a better place to work than other neighbouring factories.
23. rarely think of quitting this company.

The following points may be mentioned regarding this analysis:

(i) The communality of each test item has been taken as equal to the highest correlation in the column from that item.

(ii) Reflection had to be resorted to in the case of some items of every factor residual for maximising positive signs.

(iii) To know the point where enough factors have been taken out and further analysis should be discontinued, an empirical criterion developed by Tucker has been employed. The rule is given by the relation,

$$\emptyset = \sqrt{\frac{\Sigma Ps+1}{\Sigma Ps}} = \frac{n-1}{n}$$

Table 9

Inter-correlation of the 23 Items (N = 175)

	(1)	(2)	(3)	(4)	(5)	(6)	(7)	(8)	(9)	(10)	(11)	(12)	(13)	(14)	(15)	(16)	(17)	(18)	(19)	(20)	(21)	(22)	(23)
1		.35	.13	.15	.05	.01	.05	−.07	.05	−.15	.02	.03	−.01	.17	−.06	−.30	−.03	.04	.21	.17	.09	.01	−.29
2			.15	.26	.18	.19	.21	−.06	.14	.11	.20	−.14	.09	.29	−.02	.19	.03	.07	.13	.11	.13	.34	−.35
3				.48	.59	.36	.43	.38	.30	.22	.10	.17	.28	.28	.14	.15	.40	.29	.36	.49	.65	.41	.39
4					.56	.43	.32	.20	.34	.17	.21	.10	.28	.39	.23	.28	.68	.25	.24	.36	.49	.32	.23
5						.30	.84	.27	.23	.19	.21	.07	.25	.33	.18	−.18	.34	.35	.21	.40	.55	.37	.38
6							.54	.13	.39	.15	.06	.09	.27	.32	.19	.22	.27	.27	.18	.23	.01	.31	.18
7								.24	.52	.27	.08	.24	.34	.30	.29	−.14	.30	.44	.38	.34	.44	.44	.38
8									.29	.25	.22	.31	.39	.32	−.20	.06	.27	.30	−.32	.43	−.18	.28	.24
9										.20	.19	.30	.43	.40	.38	.52	.30	.38	.15	.41	.44	.31	.08
10											.66	.53	.32	.28	.27	.10	.08	.30	−.50	.21	.21	.18	.15
11												.58	.41	.25	.90	.07	.18	.21	.07	.32	.06	.24	−.31
12													.29	.09	.30	.11	.01	.15	.06	.25	.15	.09	.39
13														.53	.74	.38	.34	.37	.20	.42	.39	.38	.25
14															.76	.58	.24	.18	.13	.42	.34	.37	.28
15																.45	.01	.17	.04	.36	.23	.22	.16
16																	−.12	.10	−.06	.21	.21	.17	−.01
17																		.44	.38	.37	.23	.27	.08
18																			.45	.39	.41	.31	.18
19																				.42	.38	.32	.42
20																					.64	.44	.19
21																						.42	.30
22																							.30

where n is the number of test variables in the correlation matrix, ΣPs is the sum of the absolute values of the residuals after s factors and with adjusted diagonal and $\Sigma Ps+1$ is the sum of the absolute values of the residuals after $(s+1)$ factors with original or unadjusted diagonal values.

If Ø equals or exceeds $\frac{n-1}{n}$, then s is really the last factor needing extraction. In this analysis, this test was applied after the 4th factor loadings were calculated and 4th factor residuals computed. To know whether the 3rd is really the last factor, the following statistics were calculated.

$$\Sigma P_3 = 50.722; \quad \therefore \varnothing = 0.9624$$
$$\Sigma P_4 = 46.984; \quad \frac{n-1}{n} = 0.9565$$

Since ø exceeds $n-1/n$, it may be accepted that the 3rd factor is the last factor that should be extracted from this correlation matrix.

(iv) Table 10 gives the original factor loadings for the different test items.

Table 10

Factor Loadings of the 23 Test Items on the Three Centroids Prior to Rotation of Axes

	Factor loadings				Factor loadings		
Items	I	II	III	Items	I	II	III
1	.083	.207	−.238	2	.252	.127	−.407
3	.667	.309	.202	4	.654	.248	−.122
5	.642	.407	.348	6	.482	.110	−.122
7	.692	.396	.270	8	.357	−.156	−.293
9	.622	−.151	.071	10	.416	−.439	−.427
11	.498	−.548	.089	12	.406	−.442	−.380
13	.691	−.339	.078	14	.685	−.213	.284
15	.568	−.582	.391	16	.305	−.421	.279
17	.492	.265	−.109	18	.556	.126	.086
19	.368	.621	−.308	20	.703	.058	−.018
21	.619	.310	.054	22	.593	.152	−.048
23	.345	.129	.495				

Thurstone believes that if the factors should have psychological as well as mathematical meaning, and would remain invariant even if the test was analysed as part of a different battery, the centroid factors must be rotated. This is necessary not only for the first centroid which includes almost of everything that is in the battery but also for the second and subsequent factors which have positive weights on some test items and negative weights on others. In this study although only three factors have been extracted, the rotations have been done on the more general method of taking only two factors at a time, rotating them about the third axis and computing the new factor loadings after this rotation. This procedure has been repeated as many times as necessary. The location of the new axis has been guided by the principle of maximisation of zero factor loadings and minimisation of negative loadings.

Altogether three rotations had to be made. The first rotation was about Axis I, in the plane II-III, the angle of rotation being 49° (Clockwise). The second rotation of 66° was of factors I and II' around the axis III'. This was followed by a third rotation of 58° in the plane II''-III' about the axis I'. The final loadings of the test items on the three factors indicated by the symbols *C*, *Sp̂* and *Sô* are given in Table 11.

To determine the uniqueness of any factor solution, Thurstone has put forth his theory of 'simple structure'. He has laid down three empirical conditions to determine how far the factor loadings satisfy the test of 'simple structure'. These are:

(a) at least one zero loading in each row;
(b) at least as many zero loadings in each column as there are columns;
(c) at least as many XO or OX entries in each pair of columns as there are columns; by an XO entry is meant a loading in each column opposite a zero in the other.

As regards the loadings of the 23 items on the three factors arrived at after rotation (Table 11) it will be seen that conditions (b) and (c) are satisfied. But the first condition is not fully satisfied. Only 11 rows out of 23 have one zero loading each. This means that although no factor is general and the test items are qualitatively different, there are nevertheless some items in which all the three factors are present. This

Table 11

Final Factor Loadings of 23 Test Items on the Three Common Factors

Test item	*C*	*Sp̂*	*Sô*	*Communality*	*Uniqueness*
1	.173	.108	–.254	.1061	.8939
2	.239	.351	–.254	.2448	.7552
3	.728	.024	.225	.5812	.4188
4	.651	.280	.033	.5033	.4967
5	.782	–.142	.257	.6977	.3023
6	.432	.267	.046	.2600	.7400
7	.751	–.012	.284	.6448	.3552
8	.153	.461	.036	.2372	.7628
9	.393	.326	.393	.4152	.5848
10	.010	.727	.138	.5477	.4523
11	.049	.451	.593	.5575	.4425
12	.005	.690	.168	.5043	.4957
13	.329	.448	.538	.5984	.4016
14	.422	.234	.602	.5952	.4048
15	.373	.449	.152	.3638	.6362
16	–.003	.157	.569	.3484	.6516
17	.538	.186	–.034	.3252	.6748
18	.517	.144	.210	.3321	.6679
19	.647	.090	–.435	.6159	.3841
20	.579	.324	.238	.4969	.5031
21	.678	.106	.104	.4817	.5183
22	.551	.245	.117	.3773	.6227
23	.391	–.254	.404	.3806	.6194

defect has arisen in spite of all precautions taken at the time of construction of the original scale to ensure that one item refers only to one single variable or factor. How far construction of attitude items is possible such that to a large group of persons it will always have the same connotation and response to which will be dictated by reference to the same issue is a debatable question. Thus although the factor loadings of this scale do not fully satisfy Thurstone's conditions of a 'simple structure' (which even a test of mental ability seldom does) its findings are nevertheless of much practical value and fully in accord with the logical analysis of the field.

IV

Identification of the Primary Factors

"The findings of factors in an analysis simply indicates the presence of some common causes or determiners in the variables analyzed" and almost the only way of identifying them is to examine which test or test items are most highly saturated with them; in other words, on the basis of content analysis of the relevant tests. Thus the first factor, for example, in Table 11 is present to a substantial degree (accounting for more than 10% of the total variance of the item) in 16 items. These 16 items refer to the worker's satisfaction with wages, with supervision, and company policies and practices. It finds best expression in items referring to satisfaction with wages and the chances a person has got in increasing his income. It also runs through items referring to other aspects of the organisation, like the effectiveness of supervision, the company's overall pesonnel policy, its welfare activities etc. This factor, it seems, combines within itself aspects of what Katz has called identification with the company i.e., satisfactions derived from membership of the total organisation and the indirect satisfaction that he derives because of the needs that he can satisfy outside the company through the wages he gets etc. It also seems that underlying this factor and very closely associated with it is the feeling of confidence the worker has in the company, when by confidence is meant, following McGregor, "the genuine emotional conviction that one will be able reasonably to satisfy one's needs through this employment relationship". This factor has therefore been referred to as factor C.

The second and third factors in Table 11, called factors $S\hat{p}$ and $S\hat{o}$ respectively, are easier to interpret. Items carrying significant loads of these factors (of more than 0.32) refer directly or indirectly to the supervisor and the nature of supervision. A further examination of the contents of these items show some clear-cut differences between the two factors. Items highly saturated with factor $S\hat{p}$ refer to the reasonableness of the first-line supervisor in the work he expects from the worker, the attention he gives to his various suggestions, the extent to which the worker can regard him as 'his own man' the skill with which the foreman handles his workers etc. Factor *Sô*, on the other hand, is covered by items having to do with facilities given to the worker for doing his job properly, allotment and division of the work-load, the way in which his suggestions for improving methods of work, tools etc., are received and so on; in short, it has reference to the technical and organisational efficiency of the shop supervision. Factor *Sp* thus seems to refer to the human and personal aspects of supervision whereas factor *Sô* refers to the organisational and technical aspects of supervision. That workers make a distinction between these two aspects of supervision is now very much recognised.

It may be noted that a worker's liking for his job and his feeling of security at it seem to be largely determined by or related to his pesonal relations with his supervisors (factor *Sp̂*). It is again this relation he has with his boss and the treatment he receives from him that serve as an indicator to him of the way in which the company tries to treat its workers. If the boss is good, the company is good and conversely also. On the other hand, it may also be noted that the frequency with which a person thinks of quitting his job seems to be closely related to the shop organisation and the efficiency with which it is run (factor *Sô*).

The above interpretation of the nature of three factors seems to the present investigator as essentially logical. But as has been pointed out by others, the name given to a factor is merely the experimenter's hypothesis regarding the nature of that factor. Only further studies can show how far the present results are generally applicable, for these are affected to some extent by the nature of the scale, the characteristics, personal and otherwise, of the subjects, by the way of scoring of the scale etc.

V

Summary and Conclusion

Recent studies have shown that the unitary concept of morale is not adequate. Rather, morale is a multi-dimensional concept and can be broken down into a number of factors. To determine what these factors are and how they saturate the different items in an attitude scale, a factor analysis was done with data collected from a morale survey of workers in a Calcutta engineering factory. To ensure that items making up the scale used for measuring morale are valid and relevant to the workers concerned, the scale was constructed after extensive preliminary interviews and four pre-tests.

The results of the factor analysis have revealed the presence of three factors or dimension of morale. The first of these, called factor C, refers to the worker's satisfaction with the total organisation as well as with the benefits he derives from it. It refers to issues like how the factory compares with other factories as a place to work, whether the company is generally sympathetic to the workers and appreciative of their point of view, whether the income is satisfactory etc. In short, this factor refers to the feeling of confidence the individual has got in the company and the conviction he has of being able to satisfy his needs from this employment relationship.

The other two factors refer to satisfaction with supervision. The men distinguish between satisfaction derived from inter-personal relations with the supervisor as a person and satisfaction with his technical competence and running of the shop. The first factor, *Sp̂*, has reference to such items as the supervisor's skill in handling the men, his reasonableness in what he expects from them and in general, how far he can be regarded as their 'own man'. Factor *Sô* has reference to the effectiveness and competence with which the supervisor performs his duties like division of work-load, attention to workers' suggestions regarding methods of work etc., giving facilities to his men for doing the work properly and so on.

The most conspicuous among those items which have high specificity is the one that refers to how far the worker is satisfied as to his ability to do the job properly and if there is some other job which he may be able to do better. It is expected that this item may have reference to another morale dimension bound up with the nature of the job itself. Such a factor as intrinsic job satisfaction, that is, satisfaction with the nature of work itself has been isolated by other investigators.

In conclusion, it may be said that three factors isolated above together with the one referring to satisfaction with the job content do not exhaust all the possible morale dimensions. Other factors may be there. Satisfactions derived from membership of the immediate work group, from being part of an occupational system etc., have been mentioned by others. Further investigations are necessary to know how far relevant these factors are for the Indian workers and how do they load the different items. There is no reason to believe however that sources of satisfaction for the Indian workers is very much different from those of workers in other countries.

V

C, S_p And S_o Scales of Job Satisfaction

It has been said, for example, by Guilford: "As a rule, no single test can be taken as a pure measuring stick for any primary ability" and a combination of tests gives a better prediction of some single criterion. This applies also to measurement of primary attitudinal dimensions.

It will be seen from Table 11 that there are several items which carry a load of 0.35 or more (variance of 10 per cent and above) for more than one factor. Examples are items 9 and 13. On the other hand, item 3 is almost a pure measure of *C* if we ignore any load of less than 0.33; similarly, item 10 of S_p and item 16 of S_o.

In the setting up of a scale for a particular factor, items with less than 10 per cent load on that factor have been left out. For factor *Sô*, only item 16 is a 'pure' measure of *Sô*. Therefore for *Sô* scale, three other items carrying loads on the other factors have also been included.

The following items have been selected for measuring the three morale dimensions:

Factor *C*: Items 3, 4, 5, 7, 17, 18, 21, 22
Factor S_p : Items 2, 8, 10, 12
Factor S_o : Items 11, 14, 16, 23

Item 17 refers to factory canteen. In view of the wider availability of fringe benefits in contemporary industries, the term canteen may be replaced by 'Retirement, housing, and other non-medical benefits'. Mention of Factory dispensary in item 18 may similarly be replaced by 'Health Services, accident compensation, maternity leave, etc.'
Tables 12, 13, and 14 give the three scales.

Table 12

C SCALE
(Confidence in Company)

1. Do you think that the organisation's policy is to overdrive the worker and get the maximum out of him?

........1 Strongly agreed
........2 Agreed
........5 Strongly disagreed
........3 Undecided
........4 Disagreed

2. How satisfied are you with your present total earnings?

........1 Very dissatisfied
........5 Completely satisfied
........3 Neither satisfied nor dissatisfied
........4 Fairly well satisfied
........2 Dissatisfied

3. Do you think that your income is somewhat larger than what you would have got in other similar organisation?

........1 Very much less
........2 Somewhat less
........3 About the same
........5 Very much larger
........4 Somewhat larger

4. How satisfied are you with the chances you have in increasing your income in this organisation?

........5 Very well satisfied
........1 Very dissatisfied
........3 So so
........4 Fairly well satisfied
........2 Somewhat dissatisfied

5. Are you satisfied with the running of the factory canteen, housing, retirement and other non-medical benefits?

........3 Undecided
........4 Satisfied
........2 Dissatisfied

6. How do you feel about the health services, accident and maternity benefits, etc.?

........4 Services are satisfactory
........2 Services are unsatisfactory
........3 Undecided

7. Do you believe that the company/organisation is sympathetic to and appreciative of the worker's point of view?

........1 It is definitely not true
........2 In general it is not true
........3 In some cases they are sympathetic, in some not
........4 I believe this to be more or less correct
........5 I strongly believe this

8. Is this factory/organisation a better place to work than other neighbouring units?

........4 To a large extent, it is
........5 It definitely is
........3 It is about the same
........1 It definitely is not
........2 To a large extent, it is not

Table 13

SCALE S_p
(Personal Aspects of Supervision)

1. Considering your job as a whole, how well do you like it ?

........2 I do not like it much
........3 I like some things about it, dislike others
........5 I like it very much
........4 I like it fairly well
........1 I do not like it at all

2. Do you believe that so long as you work efficiently you will not lose your job?

........1 Strongly disagreed
........2 Disagreed
........3 Undecided
........5 Strongly agreed
........4 Agreed

3. How reasonable is your immediate superior in the work he expects from you ?

........2 Not very reasonable
........4 Fairly reasonable
........5 Very reasonable
........3 About average
........1 Quite unreasonable

4. Do you feel that he is your own man?

........5 Yes, he definitely is
........3 May or may not be
........4 To a large degree, he is
........2 In most matters, he is not
........1 He definitely is not

Table 14

SCALE S_o

(Organisational Aspects of Supervision)

1. Do you feel your superior gives reasonable attention to your suggestions as regards method of work, tools, equipment etc.?

........2 Disagreed
........1 Strongly disagreed
........5 Strongly agreed
........4 Agreed
........3 Undecided

2. How satisfied are you with the allotment of work in your section/department?

........1 Very dissatisfied
........2 Dissatisfied
........5 Very satisfied
........4 Satisfied
........3 Undecided

3. Do you feel you are given maximum facilities for doing your work properly?

........1 We never get any facility
........2 Mostly we do not get facilities
........4 We get most of the facilities
........3 We get about fifty-fifty
........5 We get every facility

4. Have you ever thought of quitting the services of the company?

........4 Rarely

........3 Occasionally

........2 Very frequently

VI

SCORING

1. The above three scales may be used both for industrial and non-industrial employees, by substituting the term company for factory in the items. Also, a single scale for satisfaction with supervision may be obtained by combining the two sets of S_p and S_o items, eight items in all.

2. In working out scores for respondents on the basis of a factored scale, the logical procedure is to compute the weighted values for different items measuring the factor and then combine these values. These weighted values reflect the loads of the factor. However, from a practical standpoint not much can be gained in this way. Also, information received through an attitude scale is not so precise as to justify computation of weighted scores for items. Therefore the response alternatives have been scored, as before, on a five-point (1 to 5) or a three-point (2 to 4) basis, the higher points indicating a more favourable attitude. The sum of scores of response alternatives checked by a respondent represent his factor score.

3. The three scales, *C*, S_p and *Sô* have been used on 548 workers described earlier. The means and SDs are given below:

C Scale:	16.2 ± 4.27	(Max Range 10-38)
S_p Scale:	12.2 ± 2.95	(Max Range 4-20)
S_o Scale:	13.2 ± 3.39	(Max Range 5-19)
N=548		

4. For purposes of intra-group and inter-group comparisons, standard scores with mean of 50 and SD of 10 for actual test scores are given in Tables 15, 16, and 17.

5. Norms for evaluating 'goodness' or quality of satisfaction from standard scores are given later.

Table 15

Test Scores and Standard Scores for C Scale (N = 548)

Test Score	Standard Score	Test Score	Standard Score
10	35	24	68
11	38	25	71
12	40	26	73
13	42	27	75
14	45	28	78
15	47	29	80
16	50	30	82
17	52	31	85
18	54	32	87
19	57	33	89
20	59	34	92
21	61	35	94
22	64	36	96
23	66	37	98
		38	100

Table 16

Test Scores and Standard Scores for S_p Scale (N = 548)

Test Score	Standard Score	Test Score	Standard Score
4	22	12	49
5	26	13	53
6	29	14	56
7	32	15	59
8	36	16	63
9	39	17	66
10	43	18	70
11	46	19	73
		20	76

Table 17

Test Scores and Standard Scores for S_o Scale (N = 548)

Test Score	Standard Score	Test Score	Standard Score
5	26	12	46
6	29	13	49
7	32	14	52
8	35	15	55
9	38	16	58
10	40	17	61
11	43	18	64
		19	67

CHAPTER VI

NORMS, ADMINISTRATION AND USE OF SCALES

I

Norms

Standard scores on job satisfaction derived from raw scores in the SEA, *C* and other similar scales require a classification scheme to indicate the degree of satisfaction these represent. Therefore, on the basis of five distributions of job satisfaction scores obtained by different investigators in India and covering a total sample of 1279 employees, standard score norms have been developed for placing employees in 3 to 5 categories of goodness. The details of the logic and methodology of this system is discussed elsewhere (Ganguli, 1983; pp. 74-84). Tables 18 and 19 present these norms.

Table 18

Norms for Three-way Goodness of Employee Satisfaction

Satisfaction Subgroup	Standard Scores of Job Satisfaction
Satisfied	51 and above
Middling or Average	31-50
Dissatisfied	30 and less

Table 19

Norms for Five-way Goodness of Employee Satisfaction

Satisfaction Subgroup	Standard Scores of Job Satisfaction
Highly Satisfied	66 and above
Satisfied	51-65
Middling or Average	31-50
Dissatisfied	16-30
Highly Dissatisfied	15 and less

An investigator using the 12-item SEA Scale or the *C* scale or any other employee attitude scale constructed on similar lines can, by referring to Table 18 or 19, know the degree of satisfaction of a particular employee tested. Also, if a group has been tested, the whole group can be divided into three or five satisfaction subgroups by referring to these tables. Since the tables are in terms of standard scores, the investigator has to convert the raw scores from the scale used to standard scores with a mean of 50 and SD of 10.

II

Administration of the Scales

The trustworthiness and adequacy of data sought through questionnaires or scales are a function of several variables:(1) The nature of the area being studied; for example, is it private and sensitive or is there any likelihood of harm to the person in case the information is divulged. (2) The soundness of construction of the Schedule or the Scale. (3) The personality, skill and experience of the interviewer.(4) Finally, the respondent's intelligence, education, social background etc. and his motivation or desire to cooperate with the study as well as competence to provide honest and adequate answers. It is important that the investigator takes adequate precautions to avoid errors emanating from these points.

It may be noted that the term job satisfaction does not appear in the title of the scales. The term employee attitude is a better title and may produce less of biased responses from the subject. In most studies on job satisfaction, an appropriate appeal to secure the cooperation of the subject is important. The appeal has to vary according to the socio-cultural and occupational status of the subject. The appeal, for example, may be an invitation to the subject to help improve working conditions in the organization. It may also be necessary to counteract negative motivational forces. For example, unwillingness to answer items on superior-subordinate relationship may be counteracted by assuring the respondent that data will be kept strictly confidential or if a group is being tested, then only group results will be submitted to the management. It is desirable that an outside assistant is engaged to collect the data instead of a person on the pay roll of the company.

III

Use of the Scales

Some of the uses of the SEA scale, *C* scale and S_p and S_o scales are now mentioned. (1) The scales may be used to compare different sub-groups of the same company or from different companies at one point in time. (2) The scales may be used to note the outcome of any organizational development programme through a before-and-after testing. (3) The SEA and *C* scales may be used by industrial planners to note the general satisfaction levels of employees in different regions or different industries in the country. For example, levels of satisfaction of employees of different nationalised banks in West Bengal or of employees of the same bank enjoying same pay and status and having same job conditions but located in different metropolitan cities or in urban and rural areas. Data so collected shall serve as population norms of job satisfaction of employees differing in occupation, religion, language, caste, education etc. The basic design of all such studies shall be of the sample survey research.

The clinical use of the scales for individuals suffering from emotional disorders, chronic absenteeism etc. and requiring counselling are other important applications. This is an important field and has not been adequately developed in India.

Correlational studies may provide answers to such questions as to what are the most satisfactory age, education and other personal characteristics of employees in particular jobs. Even the desirable sex, male or female, for different occupations may be known through properly designed studies with these scales. For example, in laundering and pressing work for clothes, are males to be preferred or females? Correlational studies are also useful in noting influence of trade union membership on worker satisfaction, relation of job satisfaction to nature of work, positions in the organization, to overall performance etc.

CHAPTER VII

HOW SATISFIED ARE INDIAN INDUSTRIAL WORKERS: An Example

I

Job Satisfaction of Workers

A question very often put by industrial management, is: "What percentage of Indian industrial workers can be regarded as satisfied with their job?". This type of question may seem naive to the expert industrial psychologist who is only too well aware of the numerous factors like wages, security, company personnel policy, supervision, worker aspiration, etc. that determine satisfaction with the job, factors that vary from factory to factory and in the same factory from time to time. But an answer to this is important as this can then serve as a standard by which management leaders can evaluate the significance of their own employee satisfaction figures. It is also likely to be helpful to officials responsible for planning for labour utilization and labour pacification.

One way to answer this question, therefore, is to get as many job satisfaction studies as possible and with the help of adequate statistical formulae to try to arrive at a single figure that may be regarded as indicative of percentage of satisfied workers in India in general. Fortunately, the problem has been simplified by the existence of five job satisfaction studies made in different factories in the Bengal-Bihar industrial belt. The following are the details of the five studies.

		Study conducted by
Study I	382 workers in a Calcutta engineering factory	H.C. Ganguli
Study II	548 workers in a Calcutta engineering factory	H.C. Ganguli
Study III	99 workers in a Calcutta engineering factory	K.C. Sharma and D. Sinha (1960)
Study IV	100 workers in a private steel factory	P. Sinha and D. Sinha (1960)
Study V	150 workers in a Government railway engineering workshop	H.C.Ganguli

Figure I gives the distribution of standard job satisfaction scores for the entire pooled group of 1279 workers.

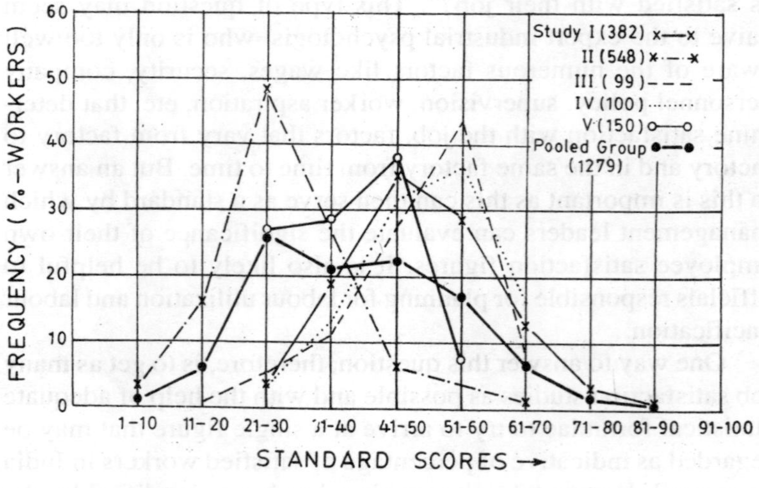

Fig. I: Job Satisfaction Scores for 1279 Indian Factory Workers.

Using the norms given in the Norms chapter, the proportion of workers in different satisfaction groups in the present sample of 1279 workers are worked out in Table 20.

Table 20

Job Satisfaction of Workers in Four Engineering Factories

(N = 1279)

	Percentage
Highly satisfied	3.4
Satisfied	19.4
Average	43.6
Dissatisfied	28.8
Highly dissatisfied	4.8

As the present sample represents workers from different engineering industries in the eastern zone of India studied by four different investigators but following the same technique of measurement, the figures in Table 20 can be generalized to some extent. This would mean that in engineering industries in India about 5 per cent of workers are "highly dissatisfied" with their total job situation, 29 per cent "dissatisfied" 19 per cent "satisfied" and 3 per cent "highly satisfied". A total of about 44 per cent of workers are neither very satisfied nor dissatisfied, but occupy the neutral zone in the satisfaction-dissatisfaction continuum.

Table 21 compares satisfaction data in three private factories with one government factory mentioned in Table 20.

Table 21

Comparison of Worker Satisfaction in one Government and three Private Engineering Factories

	Government Factory (N = 150)	3 Private Factories (N = 1129)
	%	%
Highly satisfied	3.6	3.9
Satisfied	3.6	20.9
Average	66.0	40.6
Dissatisfied	26.8	29.1
Highly dissatisfied	0.0	3.5

Compared to these three private factories, the government organization does not fare vary badly. It may be noted that although the proportion of satisfied workers is less in the government organization (7 % against 25 %), it has also less of dissatisfied workers (27 % against 33%). The peculiar feature in the government workshop is that two-thirds of its workers are lumped in the central satisfaction subgroups (neutral zone) as against only 41 per cent in the private factories. It seems that the effect of a standard set of rules and regulations are to make people neither very satisfied nor very dissatisfied. On the other hand, it seems that whether a government factory is better than a private factory from the personnel point of view connot be answered simply. A good private factory can be better than a government factory, while a backward private company can be worse. A government factory tends to give average satisfaction to the largest number of its employees.

II

Job Satisfaction of Supervisors

Supervisors are generally more satisfied than their non-supervising subordinates. Higher the cadre, greater the job-satisfaction.

Fifty per cent of supervisors in a railway workshop are satisfied and five per cent dissatisfied as compared to seven per cent satisfied and 27% dissatisfied non-supervisory workers. See Table 22 and Fig. II.

Table 22

Job Satisfaction of Supervisory and Non-Supervisory Employees in an Engineering Workshop

	Supervisory Employees (N = 87) %	Non-Supervisory Employees (N = 150) %
Highly satisfied	8.0	3.6
Satisfied	41.4	3.6
Average	46.0	66.0
Dissatisfied	4.6	26.8
Highly dissatisfied	0.0	0.0

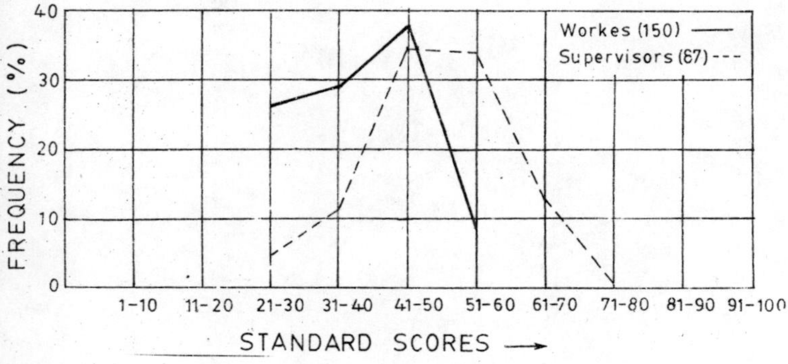

Fig. II. Job Satisfaction Scores of Supervisors and Rank and File Workers in a Government Railway Workshop.

Reference

Ganguli, H.C. *Structure and Processes of Organization*. Asia Pb. House, Bombay and reprinted by Allied Publishers, New Delhi 1983.

Fig. 11. [illegible] Supervisors [illegible] Railway Workshop.

References

Ghiselli, E.E. [illegible]

APPENDICES

SPECIMEN TEST BOOKLETS, SCORING KEYS AND NORMS

Appendix 1

Consumable Booklet
(English Version)

SHORT EMPLOYEE ATTITUDE SCALE (SEA SCALE)

Sl.No.___ Date:_______ Place:______ Organization:________

Name (Optional) .... Sex: .... Religion:..............................
Date of Birth: .... Mother Tongue: .... Highest Exam Passed:..........
Marital Status: .... No.of Children Below 18: Boys............ Girls.........
Residence upto 12: .... Urban/Semi-Urban/Rural/Mixed...............................
Present Designation: .... Duration in this:...
Permanent/Tenure/Temporary/Any Other: ....
Total Service: .... Total monthly income: Now:..........3 yrs. back:..........
Income you expect: .... Reasons:..

The objective of this study is to improve the quality of working life in this organization. Therefore knowledge of your feelings and attitude about your job is necessary. Following pages contain a number of questions on various aspects of your job. Each question carries a number of alternatives. Please read each question carefully and indicate your attitude by checking only one alternative that is most appropriate for you.

There are no right or wrong answers. Whatever reflects your personal views best is the right answer for us. Please be sure to answer all questions, without omitting any.

Your answers will be treated as strictly confidential.

There is no time limit but normally you should finish it within 30 mts.

Scale constructed and validated by: Dr H.C. GANGULI.
F 8/13 Model Town,
Delhi - 110009

TEST SCORE: CATEGORY: SS: S: M: D; DD
STANDARD SCORE: Or S: M: D:
Investigator

SHORT EMPLOYEE ATTITUDE SCALE (SEA SCALE)

1. Is there any other work you think you would be able to do better than your present work?

...........I cannot say for certain
...........I do this better than I could do most
...........Almost any other work I think I would be able to do better
...........There are a few others which I could do better
...........I am best at this work

2. Do you think that the organization's policy is to over-drive the employee and get the maximum out of him?

...........Strongly agreed
...........Agreed
...........Strongly disagreed
...........Undecided
...........Disagreed

3. How satisfied are you with the chances you have in increasing your income in this organisation?

...........Very well satisfied
...........Very dissatisfied
...........So so
...........Fairly well satisfied
...........Somewhat dissatisfied

4. Do you believe that so long as you work efficiently you will not lose your job?

...........Strongly disagreed
...........Disagreed
...........Undecided
...........Strongly agreed
...........Agreed

5. How reasonable is your immediate superior in the work he expects from you?
.... Not very reasonable
.... Fairly reasonable
.... Very reasonable
.... About average
.... Quite unreasonable

6. How much satisfied are you with the general supervision of your section/department?
.... Satisfied
.... About average
.... Dissatisfied
.... Very dissatisfied
.... Very satisfied

7. How much interest your superior or section in-charge takes in your general welfare?
.... Much interest
.... Some interest
.... Very little interest

8. Are you satisfied with the running of the canteen, housing, retirement and other non-medical benefits?
............Undecided
............Satisfied
............Dissatisfied

9. Do you believe that the company/organization is sympathetic to and appreciative of the employee's point of view?
.... It is definitely not true
.... In general it is not true
.... In some cases they are sympathetic, in some not
.... I believe this to be more or less correct
.... I strongly believe this

10. Do you feel that the company satisfies the reasonable demands of the employees?
............Strongly agree
............Agree

............Strongly disagree
............Disagree
............So so

11. Is it that this organization is a better place to work than other similar organizations?
............To a large extent, it is
............It definitely is
............It is about the same
............It definitely is not
............To a large extent, it is not

12. How satisfied you feel about the progress you have made in this organization up to now ?
............Very satisfied
............Satisfied
............Dissatisfied
............So so
............Very dissatisfied

Any other points you would like us to know about your job ? Take 10 minutes.

Now hand over the booklet to the Psychologist

For the Investigator only

Scoring for SEA Scale

1. The total score of a subject is the simple addition of the score values of the response alternatives checked. The Individual has to check all the 12 terms; no omission is allowed. In case he cannot make up his mind about a particular question, he should check the middle position carrying a score of 3. If he has omitted an item, mark it as 3.

2. The minimum and maximum possible scores in this scale are 14 and 58.

3. Odd-even reliability of SEA after Spearman-Brown correction is r=0.79. (N = 250)

4. *Validity of SEA*: Checking the validity of an attitude scale is often very difficult largely due to the lack of a proper criterion whose relation to the attitude in question is not fully known in all its aspects. That is why Vermon says: 'We may claim that when reasonable precautions are taken in constructing the test, and in obtaining cooperation from the testees, the validity should be good. And there is a large measure of scattered evidence supporting this conclusion.'

The two most factors that affect validity of a test are: (i) the internal consistency of the test and (ii) the scoring of responses and the certainty that a given response represents favourable rather than unfavourable attitude toward the issues involved. (Murphy, Murphy and Newcomb). In the SEA, careful steps have been taken in securing honest cooperation of the subjects and towards giving him every facility to discuss and express his own attitudes.

The product-moment correlations between the 12 items with each other and with the total score based on these 12 items show that the double criteria of low inter-item correlation and high item-total score correlation are met adequately by the SEA Scale. High and significant *D*-Values of each of the 12 items and the data from correlation matrix support the validity of the scale. It is thus reasonable to assume that the SEA Scale yields data that are scientifically as accurate as possible for attitudinal data and the scale is acceptably valid.

For purposes of intra-group and inter-group comparisons of satisfaction scores derived from SEA, it is not possible to use raw scores derived from it. Standard scores in lieu of raw scores permit such comparisons. Therefore raw scores of 380 employees have been converted into standard scores with a mean of 50 and SD of 10.

6. Key for scoring SEA Scale, Standard score table for conversion of raw scores and norms for satisfaction categories are given below:

Key for Scoring SEA Scale

Item	Score Values for Item Alternatives as printed
1.	3; 4; 1; 2; 5
2.	1; 2; 5; 3; 4
3.	5; 1; 3; 4; 2
4.	1; 2; 3; 5; 4
5.	2; 4; 5; 3; 1
6.	4; 3; 2; 1; 5
7.	4; 3; 2
8.	3; 4; 2
9.	1; 2; 3; 4; 5
10.	5; 4; 1; 2; 3
11.	4; 5; 3; 1; 2
12.	5; 4; 2; 3; 1

Test Scores and Standard Scores on the Short Employee Attitude Scale (SEA Scale)

(N = 380)

Test Score	Standard Score	Test Score	Standard Score
14	7	36	48
15	9	37	50
16	11	38	52
17	12	39	53
18	14	40	55
19	16	41	57
20	18	42	59
21	20	43	61
22	22	44	63
23	24	45	65
24	26	46	66
25	27	47	68
26	29	48	70
27	31	49	72
28	33	50	74
29	35	51	76
30	37	52	78
31	39	53	79
32	40	54	81
33	42	55	83
34	44	56	85
35	46	57	87
		58	89

NORMS

Standard scores on job satisfaction derived from raw scores of attitude scales require a classification scheme to indicate the degree of satisfaction these scores represent. Therefore on the basis of five distributions of job satisfaction scores obtained by different investigators in India and covering a total sample of 1279 employees, standard score norms have been developed for placing employees in 3 or 5 categories of goodness. The details of the logic and methodology of this system is discussed elsewhere (Ganguli, 1983; pp. 74-84).

Tables below give these norms.

Norms for Three-way Classification of Employee Satisfaction

Satisfaction Subgroup	Standard Scores of Satisfaction
Satisfied (S)	51 and above
Middling or Average (M)	13 to 50
Dissatisfied (D)	30 and less

Norms for Five-way Classification of Employee Satisfaction

Satisfaction Subgroup	Standard Scores of Satisfication
Highly Satisfied (SS)	66 and above
Satisfied (S)	51 - 65
Middling or Average (M)	31 - 50
Dissatisfied (D)	16 - 30
Highly Dissatisfied (DD)	15 and less

Appendix 2

Consumable Booklet
(English Version)

EMPLOYEE ATTITUDE SCALE

(The E-A Scale)

Serial No: Date: Place: Organization:

Name (Optional): .... Sex: .... Religion: ....
Date of Birth: .... Mother Tongue: .... Highest Exam Passed: ....
Marital Status: .... No. of Children Below 18: Boys.......... Girls ....
Residence upto 12: .... Urban/Semi-Urban /Rural/Mixed ....
Present Designation: .... Duration in this: ....
Permanent/Tenure/Temporary/Any Other: ....
Total Service: .... Total monthly income: Now: .... 3 yrs. back: .....
Income you expect: .... Reasons: ....
....

The objective of this study is to improve the quality of working life in this organization. Therefore knowledge or your feeling and attitudes about your job is necessary. Following pages contain a number of questions on various aspects of your job. Each question carries a number of alternatives. Please read each question carefully and indicate your attitude by checking only one alternative that is most appropriate for you.

There are no right or wrong answers. Whatever reflects your personal views best is the right answer for us. Please be sure to answer all questions, without omitting any.

Your answers will be treated as strictly confidential.

There is no time limit but normally you should finish it within 30 mts.

Scale constructed and validated by: Dr H. C. GANGULI.
F 8/13 Model Town,
Delhi - 110009

TEST SCORE — CATEGORY: SS: S: M: D: DD
STANDARD SCORE: — or :
Investigator — S: M:D

EMPLOYEE ATTITUDE SCALE
(The E-A Scale)

1. Does your job give you a chance to do the things you feel you do the best (not just liking the job)?

...... Agreed
...... Undecided
...... Disagreed
...... Strongly agreed
...... Strongly disagreed

2. How satisfied are you with the allotment of work in your section/ department?

...... Very dissatisfied
...... Dissatisfied
...... Very satisfied
...... Satisfied
...... Undecided

3. How satisfied are you with your present salary?

...... Very dissatisfied
...... Completely satisfied
...... Neither satisfied nor dissatisfied
...... Fairly well satisfied
...... Dissatisfied

4. What are your chances of being given a better type of job?

...... No chance
...... Very good chances
...... Fair chances
...... Cannot say
...... Small chances

5. Do you believe that so long as you work efficiently you will not lose your job?

...... Strongly disagreed
...... Disagreed
...... Undecided
...... Strongly agreed
...... Agreed

6. How reasonable is your immediate superior in the work he expects from you?

...... Not very reasonable
...... Fairly reasonable
...... Very reasonable
...... About average
...... Quite unreasonable

7. How much satisfied are you with the general supervision of your section/department?

...... Satisfied
...... About average
...... Dissatisfied
...... Very dissatisfied
...... Very satisfied

8. Are you satisfied that the people you work with give proper recognition to your work?

...... Agreed
...... Disagreed
...... Strongly agreed
...... Strongly disagreed
...... Undecided

9. My superior encourages me to offer suggestions for improvements in my section/department?

...... Undecided
...... Disagreed
...... Strongly disagreed
...... Agreed
...... Strongly agreed

10. Do you believe that the company/organization is sympathetic to and appreciative of the employee's point of view?

...... It is definitely not true
...... In general it is not true
...... In some cases they are sympathetic, in some not
...... I believe this to be more or less correct
.... I strongly believe this

11. Do you prefer to work with your present colleagues?

...... Strongly agreed
...... Agreed
...... Strongly disagreed
...... Disagreed
...... Uncertain

12. Do you think that the organization's policy is to over-drive the worker and get the maximum out of him?

...... Strongly agreed
...... Agreed
...... Strongly disagreed
...... Undecided
...... Disagreed

13. How satisfied are you with the method of allocation of your increments?

...... Neither satisfied nor dissatisfied
...... Satisfied
...... Completely dissatisfied
...... Completely satisfied
...... Dissatisfied

14. Do you feel your superior gives reasonable attention to your suggestions as regards method of work, equipment, books etc.?

...... Disagreed
...... Strongly disagreed
...... Strongly agreed
...... Agreed
...... Undecided

15. Do you feel that this organization treats its employees worse than other organizations?

...... Agreed
...... Strongly disagreed
...... Disagreed
...... So so
...... Strongly agreed

16. Is there any other work you think you would be able to do better than your present work?

...... I cannot say for certain
...... I do this better than I could do most
...... Almost any other work I think I would be able to do better
...... There are a few others which I could do better
...... I am best at this work.

17. Do you think that your income is somewhat larger than what you would have got in other similar organization?

...... Very much less
...... Somewhat less
...... About the same
...... Very much larger
...... Somewhat larger

18. How satisfied are you with the chances of promotion in your department?

...... Dissatisfied
...... Strongly dissatisfied
...... Satisfied
...... Strongly satisfied
...... Undecided

19. How satisfied are you with the personal development, training and quality improvement programme in this organisation?

...... Undecided
...... Satisfied
...... Very satisfied
...... Dissatisfied
...... Very disatisfied

20. What is the relation in this organization between the union (or staff association) and the management?

...... Very good
...... Good
...... Very bad
...... Middling
...... Bad

21. If you are given the same type of job under same terms and conditions in a different organization, would you quit?

...... Always
...... Never
...... Probably yes
...... May not quit
...... Cannot say

22. How adequately the existing leave rules cover your average requirements?

...... These are not adequate for our purpose
...... Though these are not quite adequate, I do not have much to complain about these
...... These are satisfactorily adequate for our purpose

23. Do you feel you are given maximum facilities for doing your work properly?

...... We never get any facility
...... Mostly we do not get facilities
...... We get most of the facilities
...... We get about fifty-fifty
...... We get every facility

24. Are you satisfied with the running of the factory canteen, housing, retirement and other non-medical benefits?

...... Undecided
...... Satisfied

...... Dissatisfied
...... Very dissatisfied
...... Very satisfied

25. How satisfied are you with the chances you have in increasing your income in this organization?

...... Very well satisfied
...... Very dissatisfied
...... So so
...... Fairly well satisfied
...... Somewhat dissatisfied

26. Taking all things into consideration, how satisfied are you with your service here?

...... Not satisfied
...... Very satisfied
...... Satisfied
...... Partly satisfied, partly dissatisfied
...... Not at all satisfied

Any other points you would like us to know about your job? Take 10 minutes.

Now hand over the booklet to the Psychologist

For the Investigator Only

Scoring for E-A Scale

1. The total score of a subject is the simple addition of the score values of the response alternatives checked. The person has to check all the items in the scale: no omission is allowed. In case he cannot make up his mind about a particular question, he should check the middling position of score value 3. If he has omitted any item, mark it as 3.

2. The minimum and maximum possible scores in the E-A Scale are 27 and 129.

3. The reliability of the scale using test-retest method was : $r = 0.90$. Odd-even correlation after Spearman-Brown's correction was $r = 0.81$. Validity of the scale was checked through the internal consistency method, that is, item analysis showing low correlations between items and high correlations between total test score and item score. This analysis was done on the basis of a correlation matrix computed from data of first 100 subjects.

4. For purpose of intra-group and inter-group comparisons of satisfaction scores of different subjects on the same or different scales, the actual satisfaction scores for 240 educated female employees have been converted into standard scores with a mean of 50 and standard deviation of 10.

5. Key for scoring E-A scale, standard score table for conversion of raw scores and norms for satisfaction categories are given below:

Key for Scoring E-A Scale

Item	Score Values for Item Alternatives as printed
1.	4; 3; 2; 5; 1
2.	1; 2; 5; 4; 3
3.	1; 5; 3; 4; 2
4.	1; 5; 4; 3; 2
5.	1; 2; 3; 5; 4
6.	2; 4; 5; 3; 1
7.	4; 3; 2; 1; 5
8.	4; 2; 5; 1; 3
9.	3; 2; 1; 4; 5
10.	1; 2; 3; 4; 5

Contd....

Key for Scoring E-A Scale (Contd.)

Item	Score Values for Item Alternatives as printed
11.	5; 4; 1; 2; 3
12.	1; 2; 5; 3; 4
13.	3; 4; 1; 5; 2
14.	2; 1; 5; 4; 3
15.	2; 5; 4; 3; 1
16.	3; 4; 1; 2; 5
17.	1; 2; 3; 5; 4
18.	2; 1; 4; 5; 3
19.	3; 4; 5; 2; 1
20.	5; 4; 1; 3; 2
21.	1; 5; 2; 4; 3
22.	2; 3; 4
23.	1; 2; 4; 3; 5
24.	3; 4; 2; 1; 5
25.	5; 1; 3; 4; 2
26.	2; 5; 4; 3; 1

Test Scores and Standard Scores in the 26-item Employees Attitude Scale (E-A scale)

Test score	Standard score	Test score	Standard score
35	15	56	32
36	16	57	32
37	16	58	33
38	17	59	34
39	18	60	35
40	19	61	36
41	20	62	36
42	20	63	37
43	21	64	38
44	22	65	39
45	23	66	40
46	24	67	40
47	24	68	41
48	25	69	42
49	26	70	43
50	27	71	44
51	28	72	44
52	28	73	45
53	29	74	46
54	30	75	47
55	31	76	48

(*Contd.*)

Test Scores and Standard Scores in the 26-item E mployees Attitude Scale (E-A scale) (*Contd.*)

Test score	Standard score	Test score	Standard score
77	48	92	60
78	49	93	61
79	50	94	62
80	51	95	63
81	52	96	64
82	52	97	65
83	53	98	65
84	54	99	66
85	55	100	67
86	56	101	68
87	56	102	68
88	57	103	69
89	58	104	70
90	59	105	71
91	60	106	72

NORMS

Standard scores on job satisfaction derived from raw scores of attitude scales require a classification scheme to indicate the degree of satisfaction these scores represent. Therefore on the basis of five distributions of job satisfaction scores obtained by different investigators in India and covering a total sample of 1279 employees, standard score norms have been developed for placing employees in 3 or 5 categories of goodness. The details of the logic and methodology of this system is discussed elsewhere.

Tables below give these norms:

Norms for Three-way Classification of Employee Satisfaction

Satisfaction Subgroup	Standard Scores of Satisfaction
Satisfied (S)	51 and above
Middling or Average (M)	31 to 50
Dissatisfied (D)	30 and less

Norms for Five-way Classification of Employee Satisfaction

Satisfaction Subgroup	Standard Scores of Satisfaction
Highly Satisfied (SS)	66 and above
Satisfied (S)	51 - 65
Middling or Average (M)	31 - 50
Dissatisfied (D)	16 - 30
Highly Dissatisfied (DD)	15 and less

Appendix 3

Consumable Booklet
(English Version)

'CONFIDENCE IN COMPANY' SCALE
(THE 'C'SCALE)

Serial No: Date: Place: Organization:

Name (Optional): .... Sex: .... Religion: ....
Date of Birth: ....,... Mother Tongue: .... Highest Exam Passed: ....
Marital Status: .... No. of Children Below 18: Boys: .... Girls: ....
Residence upto 12: ..... Urban/Semi-Urban/Rural/Mixed: ....
Present Designation: .... Duration in this: ....
Permanent/Tenure/Temporary/Any Other:..
Total Service: .... Total monthly income: .... Now:... 3 yrs. back:.
Income you expect: .... Reasons: ....

The objective of this study is to improve the quality of working life in this organization. Therefore knowledge of your feelings and attitudes about your job is necessary. Following pages contain a number of questions on various aspects of your job. Each question carries a number of alternatives. Please read each question carefully and indicate your attitude by checking only one alternative that is most appropriate for you.

There are no right or wrong answers. Whatever reflects your personal views best is the right answer for us. Please be sure to answer all questions, without omitting any.

Your answers will be treated as strictly confidential.

There is no time limit but normally you should finish it within 30 mts.

Scale constructed and validated by: Dr. H.C. GANGULI
F 8/13Model Town, Delhi -110009.

TEST SCORE: CATEGORY: SS.S.M.D.DD
STANDARD SCORE: OR : SMD

Investigator:

'CONFIDENCES IN COMPANY' SCALE
('C'SCALE)

1. Do you think that the organization's policy is to over-drive the employee and get the maximum out of him?

.... Strongly agreed
.... Agreed
.... Strongly disagreed
.... Undecided
.... Disagreed

2. How satisfied are you with your present total earnings?

.... Very dissatisfied
.... Completely satisfied
.... Neither satisfied nor dissatisfied
.... Fairly well satisfied
.... Dissatisfied

3. Do you think that your income is somewhat larger than what you would have got in other similar organisation ?

.... Very much less
.... Somewhat less
.... About the same
.... Very much larger
.... Somewhat larger

4. How satisfied are you with the chances you have in increasing your income in this organisation?

.... Very well satisfied
.... Very dissatisfied
.... So so
.... Fairly well satisfied
.... Somewhat dissatisfied

5. Are you satisfied with the running of the canteen, housing, retirement and other non-medical benefits ?

.... Undecided
.... Satisfied
.... Dissatisfied

6. How do you feel about the health services, accident and maternity benefits, etc.?

.... Services are satisfactory
.... Services are unsatisfactory
.... Undecided

7. Do you believe that the company organisation is sympathetic to and appreciative of the employee's point of view?

.... It is definitely not true
.... In general it is not true
.... In some cases they are sympathetic, in some not
.... I believe this to be more or less correct
.... I strongly believe this

8. Is this factory/organisation a better place to work than other neighbouring units ?

.... To a large extent, it is
.... It definitely is
.... It is about the same
.... It definitely is not
.... To a large extent, it is not

Any other comments you would like to make? Take 10 minutes.

Hand over the Booklet to the Examiner

For the Investigator Only

Scoring for the 'C' Scale

1. The total score of a subject is the simple addition of the score values of the response alternatives checked. The subject is not allowed to omit any item. In case of uncertainty, he may mark the middle response carrying a score of 3. Inadvertent omission of any item by the subject may be scored by the investigator as 3.

2. The scale was derived on the basis of Factor Analysis. Each item also is a 'pure' measure of factor *C*, accounting for 10% or more of the variance. Scale *C* is thus a simple and pure measure of confidence in the company. It reflects the employee's genuine emotional conviction that he/she will be reasonably able to satisfy his needs through the employment relationship.

3. The minimum and maximum possible scores on '*C*' Scale are 10 and 38.

4. The factor analysis was done with 23 most discriminating items as judged from their *D*-Values from the Master Employee Attitude Scale (MEA) of 40 items and which had odd-even reliability of 0.797 and after Spearman-Brown's correction, a full-length test reliability of 0.887. The corrected reliability of *C* Scale is 0.821 and its validity has been ensured through the entire process of step-wise construction and standardization of *C* items by factory analysis.

5. For purpose of intra-group and inter-group comparison of confidence scores of different subjects on the same or different scales, the actual *C* scores of 548 employees have been converted into standard scores with a mean of 50 and a standard deviation of 10.

6. Key for scoring the *C* Scale, standard score table for conversion of raw scores into standard scores and norms for satisfaction categories are given below:

Key for Scoring C Scale

Item	Score Values for Item Alternatives as printed
1.	1; 2; 5; 3; 4
2.	1; 5; 3; 4; 2
3.	1; 2; 3; 5; 4
4.	5; 1; 3; 4; 2
5.	3; 4; 2
6.	4; 2; 3
7.	1; 2; 3; 4; 5
8.	4; 5; 3; 1; 2

Test Scores and Standard Scores for C Scale
(N:548)

Test score	Standard score	Test score	Standard score
10	35	24	68
11	38	25	71
12	40	26	73
13	42	27	75
14	45	28	78
15	47	29	80
16	50	30	82
17	52	31	85
18	54	32	87
19	57	33	89
20	59	34	92
21	61	35	94
22	64	36	96
23	66	37	98
		38	100

NORMS

Standard scores on job satisfaction derived from raw scores of attitude scales require a classification scheme to indicate the degree of satisfaction these scores represent. Therefore on the basis of five distributions of job satisfaction scores obtained by different investigators in India and covering a total sample of 1279 employees, standard score norms have been developed for placing employees in 3 or 5 categories of goodness. The details of the logic and methodology of this system is discussed elsewhere (Ganguli, 1983: pp. 74-84).

Tables below give these norms.

Norms for Three-way Classification of Employee Satisfaction

Satisfaction Subgroup	Standard Scores of Satisfaction
Satisfied (S)	51 and above
Middling or Average (M)	31 to 50
Dissatisfied (D)	30 and less

Norms for Five-way Classification of Employee Satisfaction

Satisfaction Subgroup	Standard Scores of Satisfaction
Highly Satisfied (SS)	66 and above
Satisfied (S)	51 - 65
Middling or Average (M)	31 - 50
Dissatisfied (D)	16 - 30
Highly Dissatisfied (DD)	15 and less

Appendix 4

Consumable Booklet
(English Version)

SUPERVISION ASSESSMENT SCALES

(S_p AND S_o Scales)

Serial No: .... Date: .... Place: .... Organization: ....

Name (Optional): .... Sex:................................ Religion:..........................
Date of Birth: .... Mother Tongue: .... Highest ExamPassed:.......
Marital Status: .... No. of Children Below 18: ..... Boys : .... Girls: ......
Residence upto 12: .....Urban/Semi-Urban/Rural/Mixed: ....
Present Designation: ....Duration in this: ....
Permanent/Tenure/Temporary/Any Other: ....
Total Service: .... Total monthly income: .... Now: ...... 3 yrs. back:.....
Income you expect:.............................. Reasons:..

The objective of this study is to improve the quality of working life in this organisation. Therefore knowledge of your feelings and attitudes about your job is necessary. Following pages contain a number of questions on various aspects of your job. Each question carries a number of alternatives. Please read each question carefully and indicate your attitude by checking only one alternative that is most appropriate for you.

There are no right or wrong answers. Whatever reflects your personal views best is the right answer for us. Please be sure to answer all questions, without omitting any.

Your answers will be treated as strictly confidential.

There is no time limit but normally you should finish it within 30 mts.

Scale constructed and validated by : Dr. H.C. GANGULI.
F-8/13 MODEL TOWN,
DELHI- 110 009.

TEST SCORE : Category : SS: S: M: D: DD
STANDARD SCORE : Or : S : M: D

Investigator

SUPERVISION ASSESSMENT SCALE

Scale S_o

1. Do you feel your superior gives reasonable attention to your suggestions as regards method of work, tools, equipment etc.?

.... Disagreed
.... Strongly disagreed
.... Strongly agreed
.... Agreed
.... Undecided

2. How satisfied are you with the allotment of work in your section /department?

.... Very dissatisfied
.... Dissatisfied
.... Very satisfied
.... Satisfied
.... Undecided

3. Do you feel you are given maximum facilities for doing your work properly?

.... We never get any facility
.... Mostly we do not get facilities
.... We get most of the facilities
.... We get about fifty-fifty
.... We get every facility

4. Have you ever thought of quiting the services of this organisation?

.... Rarely
.... Occasionally
.... Very frequently

Scale S_p

1. Considering your job as a whole, how well do you like it ?

.... I do not like it much
.... I like some things about it, dislike others
.... I like it very much
.... I like it fairly well
.... I do not like it at all

2. Do you believe that so long as you work efficiently you will not lose your job ?

.... Strongly disagreed
.... Disagreed
.... Undecided
.... Strongly agreed
.... Agreed

3. How reasonable is your immediate superior in the work he expects from you ?

.... Not very reasonable
.... Fairly reasonable
.... Very reasonable
.... About average
.... Quite unreasonable

4. Do you feel that he is your own man ?

.... Yes, he definitely is
.... May or may not be
.... To a large degree, he is
.... In most matters, he is not
.... He definitely is not

Any other comments? Take 10 minutes

Handover Booklet to Examiner

For the Investigator Only

Scoring for Supervision Assessment Scales : S_o and S_p

1. Scale S_p refers to the employee's satisfaction with personal relations with his immediate superior. S_o refers to his satisfaction with the superior's competence and skill in managing the department. Further, a single measure of satisfaction with these dual and combined aspects of supervision can also be had by summating the two sets of S_p and S_o Scores.

2. Scales S_p and S_o have been isolated through a process of factor analysis of a correlation matrix of attitudinal data on 23 items selected from a Master Employment Attitude Scale (MEA) of 40 items. The 23 items were the best on the strength of high and signifcant *D*-values. The MEA had a corrected S-B odd-even reliability of 0.887. The attitudinal data for the matrix were provided by test scores of 548 employees.

3. S_p and S_o thus refer to two aspects of supervision. S_p refers to satisfaction derived from interpersonal relations with immediate superior and S_o refers to his organisational and technical competence. The employee's liking for his job and his feeling of security seem to be largely determined by relations with immediate superior (S_p). The treatment he receives from his superior appears to him to be a key indicator of the way the organisation views him. On the other hand, the frequency with which a person thinks of quitting job seems to be closely related to the effectiveness with which the department is run (S_o).

4. The sum of scores of response alternatives checked by a respondent represent his factor score. The maximum and minimum scores are :

S_p	:	20 and 4
S_o	:	19 and 5

5. For purpose of intra - and inter-group comparisons, actual raw scores of 548 employees have been converted into standard scores with a mean of 50 and a SD of 10.

6. Keys for scoring S_p and S_o scales, standard score tables for conversion of test scores and norms for satisfaction categories are given below.

7. For getting a single score on satisfaction with both technical and personal aspects of supervision, S_p and S_o scales should be scored independently and the two standard scores noted. The mean or the average of the two standard scores represent the single standard score on assessment of supervision by the employee. The norms table can be used to assess the goodness of this perception by the employee.

Key for Scoring S_p and S_o

S_o Scale		S_p Scale	
Item	Score Values for Item Alternatives	Item as Printed	Score Values for Item Alternatives as printed
1.	2; 1; 5; 4; 3	1.	2; 3; 5; 4; 1
2.	1; 2; 5; 4; 3	2.	1; 2; 3; 5; 4
3.	1; 2; 4; 3; 5	3.	2; 4; 5; 3; 1
4.	4; 3; 2	4.	5; 3; 4; 2; 1

Test Scores and Standard Scores for S_p Scale (N = 548)

Test score	Standard score	Test score	Standard score
4	22	12	49
5	26	13	53
6	29	14	56
7	32	15	59
8	36	16	63
9	39	17	66
10	43	18	70
11	46	19	73
		20	76

Test Scores and Standard Scores for S_o Scale (N = 548)

Test score	Standard score	Test score	Standard score
5	26	12	46
6	29	13	49
7	32	14	52
8	35	15	55
9	38	16	58
10	40	17	61
11	43	18	64
		19	67

NORMS

Standard scores on job satisfaction derived from raw scores of attitude scales require a classification scheme to indicate the degree of satisfaction these scores represent. Therefore on the basis of five distributions of job satisfaction scores obtained by different investigators in India and covering a total sample of 1279 employees, standard scores norms have been developed for placing employees in 3 or 5 categories of goodness. The details of the logic and methodology of this system is discussed elsewhere (Ganguli, 1983 : pp 74-84).

Tables below give these norms.

Norms for Three-way Classification of Employee Satisfaction

Satisfaction Subgroup	Standard Scores of Satisfaction
Satisfied (S)	51 and above
Middling of Average (M)	31 to 50
Dissatisfied (D)	30 and less

Norms for Five-way Classification of Employee Satisfaction

Satisfaction Subgroup	Standard Scores of Satisfaction
Highly Satisfied (SS)	66 and above
Satisfied (S)	51 - 65
Middling of Average (M)	31 - 50
Dissatisfied (D)	16 - 30
Highly Dissatisfied (DD)	15 and less